Rev. W. M. Mitchell

THE

UNDERGROUND RAILROAD

FROM

SLAVERY TO FREEDOM.

BY THE

William

REV. W. M. MITCHELL,

OF TORONTO, C.W.

Second Edition.

LONDON :

WILLIAM TWEEDIE, 337, STRAND.

MANCHESTER : WILLIAM BREMNER, 11, MARKET STREET,
AND 15, PICCADILLY.

EDINBURGH: JOHN MENZIES.

1860.

WOODFALL AND KINDER, PRINTERS,
ANGEL COURT, SKINNER STREET, LONDON.

PREFACE.

THE Author of the following work is a gentleman of colour, who was born and reared in North Carolina, United States. In early life he was left a destitute orphan, and had but few educational advantages. By the local authorities of Guildford County, in that state, he was bound apprentice to a planter, whose land was cultivated by the unrequited toil of a company of his enslaved fellow-creatures, whose labour was enforced by the whip, and whose faults, real or fictitious, were punished by torture. His master was also a heartless trader in human beings. It affords a glimpse into slave morals, that though our Author was freeborn, and, in consequence of his mother being an Indian, legally exempt from bondage, it was necessary to provide expressly, in the indenture by which he was bound, against his being kidnapped or ensnared into slavery. In this service he misspent twelve precious years of his life, and became inured to the infliction of the cruelties attendant upon man-stealing and slave-driving. During the last five years of the time, the entire management of the business

A 2

was committed to his hands. Hence he is personally conversant with all the disgusting details of plantation slave-life, of the slave-pen, and of the auction-block. It has since been a source of grief to him to recollect the part he took in ordering and superintending the harassing and flogging of men, women, and children, and in separating for life those dearest to each other, whose ties of kinship man has no power to sever. The wife and the child are still the wife and the child, how far and how long soever they be parted from husband and parent.

After leaving the unholy business, Mr. Mitchell was brought under the power of God's converting grace. The study of Christianity resulted—as it ever must, when unbiassed—in his discarding with abhorrence the iniquities inherent in slavery, which in ignorance and depravity he had assisted to perpetrate. He devoted himself from that day to the cause of the enslaved; and unto this day his devotion has continued to burn with unceasing ardour and indomitable persistency. While engaged in the ministry of Christ's gospel, he has justly regarded it an essential part of his work to promote the freedom of the oppressed, the undoing of the heavy burden, and the breaking of every yoke. Believing the enactment of the Mosaic law to involve a moral principle, which is of perpetual and universal obligation, he has endeavoured to act as answering to the voice of God, saying

unto him, "Thou shalt not deliver unto his master
the servant (bondman) which is escaped from his
master unto thee. He shall dwell with thee; even
among you, in that place which he shall choose, in
one of thy gates, where it liketh him best; thou shalt
not oppress him." (Deut. xxiii. 15, 16.) Resident
in the State of Ohio, he was for many years an active
member of a Vigilance Committee, whose business is
to aid fugitives from slavery in escaping to Canada.
This is explained in the following pages, and is done
in violation of iniquitous law, and at the risk of both
money and liberty. But it is in obedience to the will
of God, enjoined by the prophet Isaiah (chap. xvi.,
v. 3, 4):—"Bring counsel," i. e. be deliberately
united, "interpose with equity; make thy shadow as
the night in the midst of noon-day; hide the outcasts; discover not the fugitive. Let the outcasts of
Moab sojourn with thee (Oh! Sion); be thou to
them a covert from the destroyer." (Lowth's Trans-
lation.) Acting thus as a director of the so-called
"Underground Railroad," he has been a blessing to
numbers of poor creatures, whose blessing in return
has rested upon him and his fellow-directors. By a
wise man "the blessing of him that is ready to perish"
is never despised; and certainly not the loving gratitude of those who by his aid attained unto freedom,
comfort, and respectability. Amongst those whose
escape it has been his honour and privilege to pro-

mote, it will interest the reader to know, is "Eliza," of Mrs. Stowe, in "Uncle Tom's Cabin," whose passage over the ice with her lovely boy has thrilled so many millions of readers. The Rev. John Rankin, a well-known Abolitionist, whose zeal during a long life has never flagged, and who has aided in the escape of thousands of fugitives, was the first to shelter this miraculously aided woman upon her stepping on the Ohio shore of the river. He passed her on to our Author, who took charge of her for a brief period, and conveyed her into the care of another. This fact is related in the book itself. I refer to it because of the additional proof it affords, that the talented authoress of that bewitching work has recorded facts, and has not been guilty of ex-aggeration.

A few years ago, Mr. Mitchell became a missionary to the escaped fugitives in Toronto, Canada West, in the service of the American Baptist Free Mission Society—the only one of that denomination in the United States which takes proper ground in de-nouncing Slavery as a sin, and refusing to touch its proceeds. He has succeeded in gathering a large congregation of this class of persons; but their poverty, and, alas! the strength of prejudice against colour existing in that British colony, has necessitated his visit to this country to collect money to build a chapel and school-house for their use and benefit.

On his coming to me with a letter from a friend, I
rigidly examined his credentials; and being fully
satisfied with them, I have deemed it a privilege to
promote his object to the extent of my ability.
Having had the pleasure to hear him address many
audiences, I have become impressed with the importance of giving a permanent form to the principal narratives and facts he is accustomed to relate. Hence
I suggested the publishing of the book now in the
hands of the reader. The suggestion having been
cordially sanctioned by many well-known philan-
thropists, it is hoped that, by their aid and that of
others, the little work will obtain a wide circulation.
By this means good will be done. The excellent
object Mr. Mitchell has in view will be served, as the
condition and claims of the fugitives in Canada—that
interesting class of our fellow British subjects—will
become better known to those who have the means
and the will to assist them. At least a portion of
the profits of the book will be given to the building
now in course of erection, which he hopes will be the
centre of his future labours. Principally, however,
additional information will be diffused respecting that
giant 'crime—American Slavery. Introduced by us
into that country, and still sustained by our commerce, we are more closely connected with it than
any other nation. Its abolition must and will be
brought about mainly by British influence. In this

noble work English Christians must take the lead, as
they did in effecting emancipation in the West Indies.
Dr. Albert Barnes, the celebrated commentator, has
repeatedly testified that slavery could not exist one
hour if the church in that country put forth her
power. This witness is true; but I am persuaded
that the impetus must be given by the church in this
country. Our Christian merchants, manufacturers,
and artisans, those princes of wealth, enterprise,
skill, and industry, must bring their moral influence
to bear upon the four-million-fold enormity, and it
will sink beneath the pressure, but not before. Every
instrumentality tending to evoke that influence is
valuable—though apparently feeble as this little book.
" Who hath despised the day of small things ? "

> " For grains of sand the mountains make,
> And atomies infinitude."

A spark may fire a Moscow, or a mouse may tease an
elephant to death. God speed this little book, then,
and make it mighty to the pulling down of that
stronghold of satanic blood-guiltiness and woe!

    I need not add how cordially I recommend the
case of Mr. Mitchell to the beneficent of every
denomination and class. Humanity and religion are
alike interested in it. Already he has been well received, and in all instances he has elicited testimonies
of his candour, sincerity, and ability. His creden-

tials are indubitable, his reputation high, and his
speeches are thrilling. He has done good service in
behalf of the enslaved since he came to England, and
I doubt not he will yet render efficient aid before he
returns to his family and flock. I sincerely pray for
the complete success of his mission amongst us, for
his safe arrival home in due time, and for a long
future of uninterrupted prosperity in the cause of
truth and grace.

W. H. BONNER.

Trinity Chapel, Trinity Street, Southwark,
August 22, 1860.

P.S.—Out of the multitude of testimonials spontaneously borne in favour of Mr. Mitchell, I may
append the two following:—

From the *Bolton Guardian*, April 12, 1860.

"His address was delivered with great freedom and animation,
and gave proofs of mental and oratorical powers of no mean degree.
The audience frequently applauded the noble sentiments of the
speaker."

From the *St. Alban's Times*, March 1860.

"Mr. Mitchell is a popular orator, and in himself a fine speci-
men of the intellectual capacity of the coloured race. We believe
his visit to England will not only be eminently successful as regards
its special object, but also in awakening a much stronger feeling
than even now exists against slavery and the slave-trade."

EXTRACTS FROM REVIEWS
OF THE
"UNDERGROUND RAILROAD."
By the Rev. W. MITCHELL, of Toronto, C.W.

London : TWEEDIE, Strand. Price 1s. 6d.

Christian World.

The author of this valuable little book is an American, a man of colour. Many thousands have listened with peculiar gratification to the author in the course of his journeyings in this country, to procure funds for the erection of school-rooms and chapels for the poor fugitives. These will not need to be urged to welcome the book ; we anticipate their buying it with eagerness.

Morning Star.

He furnishes a great deal of valuable information respecting the iniquities of the fugitive-slave law, the escape of slaves from the Southern States, and the mysterious operations of that most ingenious as well as useful invention, the Underground Railroad. Mr. Mitchell's work contains a brief sketch of the present condition and prospects of the various coloured settlements in Canada.

Freeman.

He (the author) has been a blessing to many poor creatures, who, but for him and his coadjutors, must have been reclaimed by the odious system from which they were fleeing. The book is one that cannot be read without deep interest. It is certain likewise to increase the reader's detestation of a system which it is only wonderful that thousands of American "Christians" still support and defend.

Christian Cabinet.

The "Underground Railroad," from the pen of Rev. W. M. Mitchell, of Toronto, C.W., ought to be read by every man, woman, and child in England.

Weekly Record.

The object of this work is most commendable. It is full of anecdotes, no less true than interesting, and while the writer assigns to a few out of the many escapes the term "providential," we would suggest that, in as far as they are all instances of the power of truth, of courage, and presence of mind on the side of liberty, they are all entitled to this phrase. An admirable portrait is prefixed to this work, which we earnestly hope will secure the widest possible circulation among all who would desire freedom for the slave. Mr. Mitchell, himself a man of colour, writes calmly, but powerfully, concerning the wrongs of his people.

UNDERGROUND RAILROAD.

THE term "Underground Railroad" is perfectly understood throughout the United States and Canada, but
not generally understood in this country; therefore
it requires some explanation. The grandeur of some
things consists in their simplicity; at least such
is the case with this most wonderful of all constructed roads, which is so admirably adapted to our
purpose, and does the slave good service. This road has
been in operation a quarter of a century or more. Like
many other inventions, it has taken considerable
time to acquire its present notoriety, and almost
universal celebrity. It had its origin from the
inventive powers of a slaveholder, as will appear from
the following very obvious, yet natural circumstance.

A slave, in the State of Kentucky, came to the

conclusion that he was not a mere thing, as the law termed him, but a man with immortal destinies in common with other men: he walked upright as a man, he reasoned as a man, therefore he saw no just cause why his master should claim a divine right to him, his wife and children, and their labour. This claim gave his master another right, that is, to flog him when he felt disposed. At all events, he would try the strength of his reasoning powers, as to whether they were sufficient to guide him safe to Canada; if not, he could only return to slavery. He accordingly eloped, and his master followed in hot pursuit, to the Ohio river, which divides the slave from the free States; here he lost the track of his escaped chattel, not knowing, or having the least idea as to, the direction the slave had taken; he therefore, gave up all hope of his recovery. Being disappointed, and the loser of a thousand dollars, and having no object on which to vent his dirty spleen, he turned upon the poor Abolitionists, and said— " The d——d Abolitionists must have a railroad under the ground by which they run off niggers." The significant term "underground" emanated from this circumstance. Of course, up to the present time the slaveholders have not succeded in locating this useful road, which is therefore as much concealed from them as though it was literally under the ground; consequently it is denominated "under-

ground." And the means by which the slaves still
disappear, like the one just alluded to, beyond the
probability of recovery, so suddenly, and with such
rapid progress, we very appropriately call a railroad! This is the derivation of the term "Underground Railroad." The reader must now understand,
that the so-called railroad is a mutual agreement
between the friends of the slaves, in the Northern
States, to aid fugitives on their way to Canada.
They are taken from one friend to another, which
is done only by night, until they reach Canada; this
is the whole secret of this mysterious phrase. In
this way we convey 1200 slaves annually into Canada.
The distance which they are led in a night varies. I
have taken them twenty miles in a night, but that is
not a usual distance; six to twelve miles is more commonly the length of each journey. It is supposed by
some persons who are not sufficiently acquainted with
the policy of the American Government, that the fugitive slaves are safe from the death-like grasp of their
masters on their arrival in the free States, but to
them there are no free States, and for them there is
no safety or freedom within the jurisdiction of the
United States' Government; no, not an inch of
ground in the land of his birth, on which the slave
can claim his title to liberty. Though there are
fugitive slaves even now in the so-called free States,
their claimants are ignorant as to their whereabouts;

besides, they are protected by public sentiment in their several localities, in opposition to the Fugitive Bill, which is unparalleled in the jurisprudence of nations. Where individual liberty is only secured by public sentiment, though that sentiment may be, and sometimes is, better than the law, yet freedom under such circumstances is never safe and secure. This sentiment must, when occasion requires, yield to the rigorous demands of the law, however unjust they may be. To insure the permanent security of human freedom, we must have the sanction of law combined with public sentiment, from which law emanates. The legislatures of some States, though few, have declared the nefarious Fugitive Bill unconstitutional, and have refused the use of their prisons for the security of the slaves when arrested. This renders it more difficult to capture them, but even with these obstructions many are captured in those States. In confirmation of the assertion relative to the insecurity of escaped slaves in the free States, I adduce the first part of the sixth section of the Fugitive Bill:—

"And be it further enacted, that when a person held to service or labour in any State or territory of the United States has heretofore, or shall hereafter, escape into another State or territory of the United States, the person or persons to whom such service or labour may be due, or his, her, or their agent or attorney duly authorised by power of attorney in writing, acknowledged and certified under the seal of some legal office or court of the State or territory in which the same may be executed, may pursue and reclaim such fugitive person, either by procuring a warrant from one of the courts, judges, or commissioners aforesaid, of the proper circuit, district, or county, for the apprehension of such fugitive from service or labour; or by seizing and arresting such fugitive, where the same can be done without process, and by taking and causing such person to be taken forthwith before such court, judge, or commissioner, whose duty it shall be to hear and determine the case of such claimant in a summary manner."

Should the fugitive endeavour to find freedom in the free States, he may be pursued. If he should attempt to evade the States, and go into any territory of the United States, he is still liable to be taken; it therefore follows he is nowhere safe in that Republic. Such fugitive, we see, may be arrested without first obtaining a warrant from the court, judge, or commissioner, without at all overstepping the bounds of legal authority. He is to be taken forthwith before such tribunals as are herein mentioned, giving the criminal no chance whatever to extricate himself.

Still adding insult to injury, his case is to be heard and determined in a "summary manner," that is,

without indictment, or even the benefit of a jury in
open court, the delivery of the verdict by the judge.
These are denied him. But beyond this mean,
unjust, and wicked encroachment on human rights,
the criminal is not allowed to raise his voice, even
in his own defence, on his trial, as I shall show
from another portion of the sixth section of the
aforesaid Bill :—

"In no trial or hearing, under this act, shall the
testimony of such alleged fugitive be admitted in
evidence. And the certificates in this and the first
section mentioned, shall be conclusive of the right
of the person or persons in whose favour granted, to
remove such fugitive to the State or territory, from
which he escaped."

Notwithstanding this prohibition and denial of
human rights, I have often heard the judge ask the
slave if he owned the claimant as his master, and
was willing to return with him into slavery. The
slave, frightened almost out of his wits, for perhaps
he had never before appeared in any court, and to
make the matter go as easy as possible with him
when he reached his former home, answers in the
affirmative. The unjust judge, for such he truly is,
takes advantage of this answer, and delivers up
the slave under the pretence that it is consonant
with the desire of the fugitive. It is considered
mean and contemptible for an individual to take ad-

vantage of his superiors, but it is infinitely more so to take advantage of the weak and helpless, especially when the answer of the poor fugitive, either in the affirmative or negative, would not affect his condition, it being previously determined with the law, as well as public opinion, by which he is doomed to return into hopeless bondage.

The glowing hope which kindled in his bosom while on his journey to a land of freedom, which also inspired him to press on with vigour, a smile occasionally beaming from his manly countenance at the pleasant thought of soon being free in a country in which he would be recognized as a friend and a brother,—all these are blasted ; hope no longer invigorates his soul, and the pleasant thought of claiming his own right to freedom no longer exists in his palpitating heart.

In the Northern States, the slave has many Christian friends, who would, in absence of law, run any risk to rescue him. Many do even now so far disregard the law as to rescue the fugitive. I cannot say I am clear of this fault, if a fault it be. To prevent this, however, the infamous Fugitive Bill has the following clause, sect. 7 :—

" And be it further enacted, that any person who shall knowingly and willingly obstruct, hinder, or prevent such claimant, his agent, or attorney, or any person or persons lawfully assisting him, her or them,

B

from arresting such fugitive from service or labour,
either with or without process, as aforesaid; or shall
rescue or attempt to rescue such fugitive from service
or labour, from the custody of such claimant, his, or
her agent or attorney, or other person or persons, lawfully assisting as aforesaid, when so arrested, pursuant
to the authority herein given and declared; or aid,
abet, or assist such person so owing service or labour
as aforesaid, directly or indirectly to escape from such
claimant, his agent, or attorney, or other person or
persons legally authorized as aforesaid; or shall harbour or conceal such fugitive, so as to prevent the
discovery and arrest of such person, after notice or
knowledge of the fact that such person was a fugitive from service or labour as aforesaid, shall, for
either of the said offences, be subject to a fine not
exceeding one thousand dollars, and imprisonment
not exceeding six months, by indictment and conviction before the district court of the United
States, for the district in which such offence may
have been committed; or before the proper court
of criminal jurisdiction, if committed within any
one of the organized territories of the United States.
And shall moreover forfeit and pay by way of civil
damages, to the parties injured by such illegal conduct, the sum of one thousand dollars for each fugitive
so lost as aforesaid, to be recovered by action of
debt, in any of the district or territorial courts as

aforesaid, within whose jurisdiction the said offence
may have been committed."

These provisions are rather prolix in their details.
Should you even attempt to rescue the fugitive, directly or indirectly, for the said offence you are subject to the penalties therein mentioned. This law is
unparalleled in the history of nations, and especially
Christian nations. God has commanded us to assist
the poor and needy, the helpless, the outcast, and
the down-trodden. In the law which God delivered
to Israel when she assumed an independent position
among the nations of the earth, He made a provision
for the fugitive slave. He commanded, first of all,
that Israel should not turn him back or deliver
him to his heathen master from whom he had fled.
She was taught her duty towards the fugitive, evidently showing that the slave was quite justifiable
in the attempt to obtain his freedom, consequently
it would be wrong for Israel to deliver him up. As
right and wrong are in opposition to each other,
both cannot be right, though one must be. If
the slave has a right to run away, he has a right
also to remain away. And if so, it is the duty of
those to whom he flees to protect him in the free and
unrestrained exercise of this acknowledged right,
which God plainly intimates in the text, Deut. xxiii.
15 and 16: " Thou shalt not deliver unto his master
the servant which is escaped from his master unto

thee: he shall dwell with thee, even among you, in
that place which he shall chose, in one of thy gates,
where it liketh him best: thou shalt not oppress
him." It was the duty of the Israelites to retain
him within their commonwealth, though the master
should have pursued him even to their very gates.
God has forbidden his delivery. He must be obeyed,
and duty strictly discharged at all hazards. The
language is imperative and unequivocal, cogent and
commanding,—" Thou shalt not deliver the servant to
his master," &c. This slave had the freedom of
choice to " dwell where it liketh him best, within thy
gates." He was to remain upon principles of perfect
equality. " Thou shalt not oppress him."

This portion of the Word of God, as well as other
portions, is shamefully trodden under foot in the
Northern States, by rendering up fugitive slaves.
The immorality does not consist in the character of
the persons to whom they are delivered, whether they
are heathen, pagan, or Christian masters: the command is, " Thou shalt not deliver the servant to his
master; " evidently implying, that whatever his character may be, the simple act of delivering him to his
master is contrary to a Divine command, and will be
punished as other wrongs, in proportion to its mag-
nitude. Wickedness is systematically framed by law,
and it is truly a fact, "men love darkness rather than
light because their deeds are evil." " Is not this the

fast that I have chosen, to loose the bands of wickedness, to undo the heavy burdens, and to let the
oppressed go free, and that ye break every yoke?"
These are perfect safeguards to human liberty, which
God has raised for the protection of the weak.

The progress of the slave is very much impeded
by a class of men in the Northern States who are too
lazy to work at respectable occupations to obtain an
honest living, but prefer to obtain it, if possible,
whether honestly or dishonestly, by tracking runaway
slaves.   On seeing advertisements in the newspapers
of escaped slaves, with rewards offered, they, armed
to the teeth, saunter in and through Abolition communities or towns where they are likely to find the
object of their pursuit.   They sometimes watch the
houses of known Abolitionists.   Their presence causes
some excitement, for it is an unmistakable indication
that the slave has left his prison-house of bondage for
Canada, where he can stand erect as a man, and claim
his own freedom, none daring "to molest or make him
afraid." We are hereby warned, and for our own safety
and that of the slave we act with excessive caution.
The first discoverer of these bloodhounds communi-
cates their presence to others of our company, so as
to put the entire band in that locality on their guard.
If the slave has not reached us, we are on the look-
out, with greater anxiety than the hunters, for the
fugitive, to prevent his falling into the possession of

those demons in human shape. On the other hand, should the slave be so fortunate as to be in our possession at the time, we are compelled to keep very quiet, until the hunter loses all hopes of finding him, and therefore gives up the search as a bad job, or moves on to another Abolition community, which gives us an opportunity of removing the fugitive further from danger, or sending him towards the North Star: the latter we prefer, as it is the safest plan for both parties. We also have patriotic men, white and coloured, voluntarily going into the slave States and bringing away their fellow-men; some of these venturous men having themselves been slaves, they are truly desirous their brethren should taste the sweets of freedom. They bring them into the free States and deliver them to the conductors of our Railway, whose duty it is to forward them to Canada. My house was for several years one of the stations to which numbers were brought by these good men. No class of men are better prepared for this perilous and dangerous occupation than fugitives themselves. First,—they are used to night-walking from their childhood. Secondly,—they are better acquainted with their own neighbourhood, to which they generally resort, to secure the freedom of their friends and acquaintances. Thirdly,—they sympathize with their brethren to a greater extent than others possibly can, from their identity with them; they are

brethren in tribulation. These men must be patriotic,
when they jeopardize their own freedom—

"Freedom lost so long, now repossess'd "—

sweet as it is, for others; this is, indeed, carrying out
the great law of love, "Whatsoever ye would men should
do unto you, do ye even so to them." I have known
instances, of which we shall speak hereafter, where they
have absolutely forfeited their own freedom, when
unfortunately overtaken with their company within
the boundaries of the slave States. A personal friend
of mine is now in prison for ninety and nine years, in
the State of Kentucky, for leading away eight slaves,
being caught within the limits of that State: a man
guilty of no crime but assisting his brethren peaceably in regaining what was unjustly taken from them.
" Behold, the arm of the Lord is not shortened that it
cannot save, neither his ear heavy that it cannot hear.
But your iniquities have separated between you and
your God. Your sins have hid his face from you,
that He will not hear, for your hands are defiled with
blood. They trust in vanity and speak lies." This
prophecy is verified in their case; their hands are
defiled with the blood of that poor man; their sins
have truly caused God to hide his face from them.
When God shall uncap the magazine of his wrath,
and the red arm of vengeance shall seize the fiery
sword of justice, and dash athwart the angry sky,

these wicked men will wake up, as from an ominous
dream, to a deep sense of justice and humanity; but,
alas! too late to retract: "the great day of his wrath
has come, and who will be able to stand?" The righteous only,—the redeemed slave in common with
others, who, in this world of wickedness and human
depravity, have worn handcuffs, will then bear palms
of victory; instead of stripes, robes of righteousness;
for scanty meals, inexhaustible festivities; instead of
their humble cabins, which no one condescends to visit
but their fellows and their drivers, they will look
abroad on the flowery plains of eternal blessedness:
their companions will be good old Abraham, Isaac, and
Jacob, all the apostles and their associates who have
fought the good fight, and have kept the faith, and are
now receiving their reward.

In 1852, by an Act of Congress, heavy penalties
were imposed upon all persons who knowingly enter-
tained or aided a fugitive slave, or, in other words, had
sufficient compassion to "feed the hungry or clothe
the naked." It was also made the duty of the United
States marshals, and all good citizens, to assist in re-
taking fugitives. Even in the slave States, the negro
hounds and the hunters are great terrors to prevent
the escape of slaves, as the following extract from the
Onachita Register of June 1, 1852, will exemplify:—

"The undersigned would respectfully inform the
citizens of Onachita, and adjacent parishes, that he

has located about two miles and a half east of John White's, on the road leading from Monroes to Bastrope; and that he has a fine pack of dogs for catching negroes. Persons wishing negroes caught will do well to give him a call. He can always be found at his stand, when not engaged in hunting; and, even then, information of his whereabouts can always be had of some one on the premises. Terms, 5 dollars per day and found, when no track pointed out; when the track is shown, twenty-five dollars will be charged for catching negroes.—M. C. GOFF. Monroes, Feb. 17, 1852."

I was initiated into this underground business in the county of Ross, in the State of Ohio, in 1843, and continued in the office, faithfully discharging the duties, until 1855. Never, for one moment, have I regretted being thus engaged, though I experienced many very unpleasant things during that period. "But God knows how to deliver his own out of temptation." Many are the times I have suffered in the cold, in beating rains pouring in torrents from the watery clouds, in the midst of the impetuosity of the whirlwinds and wild tornadoes, leading on my company,—not to the field of sanguinary war and carnage, but to the glorious land of impartial freedom, where the bloody lash is not buried in the quivering flesh of the slave, nor where the voice of prayer, and the songs of Zion, mingle with the clanking of handcuffs, the rattling of chains, the stifled groans of bereaved wives, and the piercing cries of orphan children, ascending together to the skies; where the sound of the one is drowned in the sound of the other. In this land, sacred to freedom, the poor fugitive can stand erect, and claim his own liberty, and worship his God "under his own vine and fig-tree, where no one dares to molest or make him afraid."

In 1843, I had an occasion, for the first time, to try my skill in my new profession, which was to me, I must confess, quite an awkward business; it is, however, to be hoped that my zeal and love for human freedom amply made up for this defect. Some time previous to my acquaintance with this community, a slave had made his escape from the State of Maryland, and located in this county, supposing himself secure from the clutches of his proud and self-important tyrant master; he, therefore, became content to remain protected only by public opinion. In this unmolested condition he remained for several years in connection with the Methodist congregation, and I believe he was a very useful member. His minister, probably wishing to increase his salary by the reward of 100 dollars, which was offered for the slave, or for intelligence of his whereabouts, betrayed him. While engaged in his daily avocation, by which he made an honest and respectable living for his family (he being a married man), three men came suddenly upon him, put a rope round his neck, and unceremoniously dragged him beyond the limits of the town authorities, and on to his former place of slavery, leaving a wife and three children to lament their bereavement.

The news spread, almost with lightning speed, through the coloured community. We rallied, 200 strong, in little or no time, augmenting as the news continued to spread from house to house ; men and women were much excited, and on the wing of flight in hot pursuit, some of the latter consoling the bereaved wife and children, others following the accumulating multitude to witness our success or failure, and, if necessary in order to secure the freedom of the fugitive, to lend assistance. We, however, came upon these menstealers three miles from the town. One end of the rope was attached to the neck of a horse, and the fugitive was walking or running, while the men were riding. The advancing crowd raised a shout; the slave looked behind, and motioned his hand for us to hasten our speed, but we were going at the top of our speed. When it became apparent to them that their own liberty and security were in danger, the men cut the rope from the neck of the steed, and, spurring their horses, were soon out of our reach and sight. The fugitive was borne back on the shoulders of his friends with triumphant shouts. A man saved from slavery ! The broken heart of a woman healed! For reasons best known to themselves, they never made a second attempt to enslave him, which I think, upon the whole, was as much to their own advantage as to that of the fugitive. A much-admired Christian poet has well expressed a sentiment which, I am sure, we must all admire and love :—

> " How long shall men, by Christ redeem'd,
> As beasts of burden be esteem'd ;
> And those, by grace Divine renew'd,
> Be doom'd to hopeless servitude ? "
>
> J. CONDER.

ᚠ I was eventually located in another portion of the same State ; here my home became more permanently the place for concealing the flying fugitive, and for those conducted there. Here it was I witnessed remarkable specimens of heroism in the person of an escaped slave, who had five years previously fled from the State of Kentucky to Canada, and then and there determined to devote his life to the vital interest of his brethren, by redeeming as many as possible from the undying grasp of the greedy monster, the slaveholder. He was willing to risk the forfeiture of his own freedom, that he might, peradventure, secure the liberty of some. He commenced the perilous business by going into the State from whence he had escaped, and especially into his old neighbourhood, decoying off his brethren to Canada. The morality of this business may be questioned by some, but we will consider it from a practical point of view.

Suppose you were a slave, and to secure your freedom you had escaped to Canada or elsewhere, leaving a wife and children in slavery, loving them in that condition as you do in your present condition of freedom, without money to purchase them, or if you had it, perhaps the owner would not sell them. Would it be morally wrong, if in your power, to secure their freedom by stealing them and conducting them into a land where you could live an undivided family, with the privilege of educating and bringing up your children in the fear and admonition of the Lord? If morally right to steal one slave, it is morally right to steal an indefinite number. The word steal is not a proper term to apply to this subject; I use it with the meaning only of conducting slaves, with their voluntary consent, without the knowledge of their owners, into freedom. The above question must be decided by the reader, if decided at all, in accordance with this view.

This slave brought to my house, in nineteen months, 265 human beings, whom he had been instrumental in redeeming from slavery, all of whom I had the privilege of forwarding to Canada by the Underground Railroad, as explained at the commencement.

He kept no record as to the number he had assisted in this way, but I have been able, from conversations with him on the subject, to ascertain about 1300 whom he delivered to Abolitionists to be for-

warded to Canada. Poor man! he was finally captured
and sold. He had been towards the interior of Kentucky, about fifty miles; and while returning, with
four slaves, he was captured. On one side the Ohio
River is Kentucky, a slave State, and on the other
side of that river is a free State, this river being
the dividing line. Daylight came on them; they concealed themselves under stacks of Indian corn, which
served them for food, as well as a protection from the
weather and passers-by, waiting till the sun should
go down, and leave behind him a black garment over
the face of Nature. Late in the afternoon of that
day, in the distance, was heard the baying of the
negro-hounds, on their track; escape was impossible.
To plunge into the river was to find a watery grave.
To turn back was to walk into the lion's den. Self-
defence was the only alternative; perhaps they might
cause the enemy to retreat, if not too many for
them. When the four slaves saw their masters,
they said, " J. M., we can't fight." He endeavoured
to rally up their courage, and arouse their ambition, by urging the justness of their cause, but to
no purpose. ' Their manhood had been crushed out
by the overpowering influence of slavery, brought
to bear on them through the agency of white men,
whose chains they had worn, and whose stripes
they had felt. Our hero was deserted in time of
great necessity: these cowardly slaves quietly stood,

at the command of the tyrants, until fettered with handcuffs and chains. Their leader resisted, till both his arms were broken, and his body otherwise abused. When conquered, and fairly in their possession, all hopes of escape fled; Freedom was to him as a morning's dream. On opening the eye her beautiful form disappeared; and in her stead was the frightful ghost of Slavery, looking him directly in the face. With broken arms and a mangled body, cold iron encircling his manly frame, with a heart yet beating for liberty, placing no value upon his existence, throwing back his broad shoulders, his chest projecting, said, "Put a ball in that! I don't wish to live any longer. I have taken away hundreds of slaves. Kill me; if my men had fought, I would have saved them." Though he had changed his name, as most slaves do on running away, he told his master's name, and to him he was delivered. He was eventually sold and taken to New Orleans, more than 1000 miles from where he then was, and not less than 1800 miles from Canada. Yet in one year, five months, and twenty days, I received a letter from this man, John Mason, from Hamilton, Canada West. Let a man walk abroad on freedom's sunny plains, and having once drunk of its celestial "stream whereof maketh glad the city of our God," afterwards reduce this man to slavery, and there it is next to an impossibility to retain him.

Slavery! That single word, what volumes does it speak! It speaks of chains, of whips and tortures, compulsive labour, hunger and fatigue, and all the miseries our frail bodies can suffer. It speaks of haughty power and insolent commands, of insatiate avarice, of pampered pride and purse-proud luxury, and of the cold indifference and scornful unconcern with which the oppressor looks down upon his victims. It speaks of crouching fear, though John Mason had none, because he was a superior man, above the level of his race. It speaks of low, mean cunning, and treacherous revenge, which it entails upon its vassals. It speaks of humanity outraged and manhood degraded; the social charities of life, the sacred ties of father, wife, and child, trampled under foot; aspirations crushed, hope extinguished, and the light of knowledge sacrilegiously put out. It speaks of man deprived of all that makes him amiable or noble,—stripped of his soul, and sunk into a beast. There it leaves him, in the prison-house of ignorance, a ghost-like form. To this fate their children are born. May Heaven have mercy on them, for man has none!

> "And shall the nations dare to hold
>   In chains, whom Thou hast charter'd free?
> Or buy, with their accursed gold,
>   The sinewy arm and servile knee?
> Whate'er of crime, whate'er of woe,
>   Europe has wrough and Afric wept,

In his recording volume, lo !
  The Angel of the Court has kept.
In that great day, when Afric's race
  Are from their house of bondage cast,
Oh, hide us in some peaceful place,
  Till all thy wrath be over-past."

J. H. WIFFEN.

It is often urged, though falsely, by the American slaveholders and their abettors, that the negro race does not possess, to the same degree as the white race, those strong social feelings and filial affections which lie at the foundation of human society; the essential elements and spontaneous out-growth of our nature; the potent ligaments of the whole social fabric. And as these qualities are developed, man ascends higher in the scale of intellectual, moral, social, and religious being. That these qualities are not developed in the negro equally with the white race, I readily admit. But that the negro does not possess them to the same degree as the white race, as characteristics of human nature, and that they are not capable of as high a degree of development in the negro as in the white race, I am not at all prepared to admit. Whether they possess them or not, a few examples will demonstrate. Stern facts are more cogent upon the human mind than fine-spun, hair-splitting logical arguments; though on scientific subjects these are allowable, and in many respects necessary. I had, at one time, a

C

woman with her child at my house, on her way to
Canada. It being my duty, as well as part of my
profession, to assist her, I sent a message to one of
our conductors, some six miles distant, that I should
pay him a visit that evening, for what purpose he
quite understood, as the sequel will show. Late in
the night, when the hum of business had gradually
sunk into dead silence, and the foot of the busy traveller was no longer heard, I arose from my bed,
leaving my loved ones sound asleep; then kissing
them, I threw around me an overcoat to protect me
from the cold north wind, and turning my face towards
this poor woman, I felt it was my duty as a father,
my duty as a Christian, to save this mother and her
babe from the iron grasp of slavery, if in my power.
If I ever felt the outbursting of a father's affections,
and influenced by these feelings to assist a slave-mother in securing the freedom of her darling babe, it
was then. My wife gave the child to me, and I
walked out to the gate. After looking this way and
that way we proceeded. Our steps were quick and
cautious, our words few and seldom, and rising only
to a whisper. The dead silence was now and then
broken by the bark of a neighbour's dog, at a distance. The darkness was augmented by the dim
forest into which we were suddenly to plunge, a
place pre-eminently suited for an enemy to lie in
ambush. The woman pressed close to my side as she

walked, at times walking on her toes. Occasionally a
deep sigh and a stifled groan emanated from her heaving bosom. Just here we saw, in the distance, a man
approaching us on horseback, whom she took to be an
enemy. She ran a few paces, but, returning, crouched
by my side, trembling as in the arms of death itself,
pleading for her child with the resistless power of a
woman's eloquence, in a soft and plaintive tone, in
which the power of woman's eloquence principally
consists. Under other circumstances I should have
been overcome. Again she started, but returned as
before, and said, "For God's sake give me the child."
Something like a determination spontaneously arose
in my mind. I was as ignorant as herself as to whom
we were meeting. I replied, "No one man can take
you; stick to me like a heroine." Her steps grew
steady, and her fears began to subside. To her my
counsel was "a word in season:" its effect was much
more powerful than I anticipated: it proceeded from
the impulse of nature. To our delight and surprise
(to me as well as to her), it was the gentleman to
whom we were going; he, having received my message, was coming to meet us.

Here was a fair test of a mother's affections. It
was literally impossible for her to leave her child,
though at the peril of her own life; her attempts
were to no avail. How like a mother! Could any
white mother have done more than this woman

did? Here is the strongest evidence possible of parental affection existing in the bosom of an uncultivated slave. "Out of one blood has God created all men to dwell on the earth,"—made of one common material, having one common nature, subject to one common code of laws, with equal immortal destinies, amenable to the same God, redeemed (if redeemed at all) by the same dying Saviour. The conclusion is therefore obvious, that the negro is as capable of loving and hating to the same degree as any other race of people. They that think the contrary, are [either] prejudiced against the race, or ignorant of human nature. This woman, as have many others, reached Canada safely.

As another instance of affection in the coloured race, I mention that of a company of eight slaves, who were making their way to Canada, under the guidance of one of our men, who devote their lives to that business. He concealed them at a distance of twenty miles from my house. It was in the month of January, and consequently very, very cold, and the ground was covered with snow. Among the company were two women, one a mother with three children; the other had no child. I hired a wagon, and went with this conductor the following evening to their place of concealment; on nearing the place, he took me through a forest, when, only a few roods off the party, I heard a child cry. We found them

nearly frozen. The mother's feet were so frost-
bitten that she could scarcely walk, and but for the
excitement natural to her position, she would have
considered it impossible to walk. The children
had suffered less, because the mother had deprived
herself of every comfort to protect them from the
cold. This conduct is an incontestable evidence
of a mother's love, though she be black! We
wrapped them in blankets, which we took for the
purpose, and put them in our wagon, and conveyed
them to my house. On the following evening, those
who were able were conducted on their way. The
mother and her three children remained at my house,
she being totally disabled. I employed a doctor for
her, who amputated one of her feet, but to no saving
effect. She died in the full triumph of Christian
faith. A few minutes before departing this life, she
said, in a low tone of voice, "Will you see that my
children are free?" Here was a mother's undying
affection obviously manifested in a dying body. She
loved freedom. She was much grieved because unable to pay me for my services. Occasionally, when
feeling a little better, she would say, "If I am
spared to reach Canada, I will work hard, and send
money to pay you." This showed a truly good and
great heart. I need scarcely add, that all her children are in Canada. She died in a good cause.
There is nothing greater and of more value to a human

being than religion and human liberty. She was endeavouring to secure to her children the advantages of both: to accomplish this, she sacrificed her own life. But by this sacrifice she obtained those advantages for her beloved ones, and died in freedom herself. Had she not run away, her children might have been slaves to-day, whereas they are free. This good mother is one redeemed from the galling yoke of unmitigated inhuman chattelism, and has gone through great tribulation, to join those who have "washed their robes and made them white in the blood of the Lamb."

"Hark, from heaven a voice proclaiming
    Comfort to the mourning slave ;
God has heard him long complaining,
    And extends his arm to save.
Proud oppression soon shall find its destined grave."

Another interesting case is that of a slave mother, who fled from the dark dungeon of slavery in Virginia. Learning that she was to be sold from her daughter and grandchild, though advanced in years, it seems she had an instinctive love for freedom, and attempted to achieve it by running away. During the night she travelled, concealing herself in the day-time; otherwise she might have been betrayed, taken back or lodged in gaol. Her only subsistence was Indian corn, on which she lived during her perilous journey. Mothers of England! imagine the suffer-

ing of this mother; put yourselves in her position;
no one to whom to tell her sorrows and pour out her
soul. But God, whose eye never sleeps, and whose
ears are never dull of hearing, mysteriously guided
the fugitive unto freedom. He heard and answered
her prayers. Trusting in the God of Israel, her
trembling limbs bore her feeble body northward;
subject to rain, hail, snow, and impetuous storms; a
pilgrim, not to the Holy Land, to bow to the Popish
shrine, but to freedom's land, to worship God, and
enjoy the boon of liberty, which she purchased at
almost an inconceivable price. Ascending and descending mountains, making her way through dense
forests, wading creeks, she eventually arrived in the
Key-stone State (as we call it), Pennsylvania. Seeing
in the distance a light, she approached it cautiously,
necessity compelling her to seek human aid; starvation looking her in the face, tattered rags, wearied
limbs, relaxed muscles, and sunk ambition, were
Nature's admonitions—were so many voices warning
her of the importance of temporal comforts. She
saw before her a huge form. She came to a stand-
still, endeavouring to make it out. A voice came
from it,—"Thee need not be afraid, it is a friend."
She recognized the voice of a Quaker. He took her
into his house, true as they always are to the dictates
of humanity, and the precepts of our religion; he fed,
clothed, and sheltered her. She remained in his

family some time, they being Abolitionists. She consulted the Quaker as to the propriety of attempting to rescue her daughter and grandchild from slavery. He considered her too old, the distance too great, the difficulties to be overcome more than she was capable of, besides the liability of forfeiting her own freedom; he, therefore, would not recommend her to attempt it. This advice, coming from an honest heart, was truly discouraging to her; nothing but a mother's love could have borne the burden of a broken-hearted mother. Can a mother forget the child she bore? No! not while she remains a mother. She consulted other friends, and received similar advice. Notwithstanding, being provided with food and clothing, she made her way back, by the providence of God, a distance of four hundred miles, in the direction she came, through all kinds of weather. When her stock of provisions was exhausted, she fed, as before, on Indian corn.

Approaching the habitation of the hissing serpents, they (feeling an instinctive right to defend their domiciles) warned the wearied traveller by their sound; nocturnal howls, the barking of the wolf-dog, the noise of insects, all alike familar to her ear. She arrived at her destination, and concealed herself in a wood from whence she could overlook her daughter's humble cabin; seeing negro children playing in the yard, she accosted them, and sent them to inform her daughter of her arrival, who instantly went to her mother in the forest. Their interview can be better imagined than described. The escape was planned, and thus her daughter and son-in-law were rescued from oppression's heavy hand, and led, in the same direction, to freedom's land. With light hearts they reached the good Quaker's dwelling, and were received with his usual kindness. It was some time before she could convince him that she had been back, and but for the corroborative evidence of her relations, she would probably have failed to convince him. He, as before, fed and clothed them, and they had a free passage to Canada by the Underground Railway. This narrative may appear marvellous, but it is a fact, for I am dealing with facts only.

No human being on earth could give stronger evidence of a mother's affections than this woman. It is a confirmation of what Cowper says, which, though so often recited, never loses its strength and beauty:—

> "Fleecy locks and black complexions
> Cannot forfeit Nature's claims ;
> Skins may differ, but affections
> Dwell in white and black the same."

Poor woman, born in a so-called country of freedom, gave birth to a beloved one, whom all regarded as the gift of our heavenly Father. Like her white sisters, she loved it, but, unlike them, had no acknow-

ledged rights; unlike them, she was rearing it for
the auction-block, to be sold as the calf from the
cow, to work on the cotton plantations, there to be
mangled and butchered at the will of the owner.
May Heaven have mercy on these people!—the bowels
of human sympathy seem closed to their piteous cries
and bitter wailings. The American people listen with
eagerness to the report of wrongs endured by distant
nations, which is all well enough. The Hungarian,
the Italian, the Irishman, the Jew and the Gentile,
all find in that land a home, and when any or all of
them wish to speak, they find hearts to sympathize
and ears to hear. The fugitive slave has no home
this side the grave in that republic; they will not
allow him to pass peaceably through the free States
of that glorious republic, to find a home beyond the
land of his birth, in a more favoured country, where
equal rights and privileges are allowed as the essential
properties of human nature. The soil of America has
been cultivated by slaves for centuries, and they have
performed for their masters the humblest services,
and by the labour of their sable and sinewy arms the
greatest comforts and luxuries of the slaveholders
have been gained from the earth. Among such a
people, and with such recommendations to favour, they
are esteemed less than strangers and sojourners,—
aliens in their native land. From the judicial seat of
that mighty Government comes the shameful, dis‑

graceful, wicked, and diabolical decision,—" No person, along whose veins courses one drop of African blood, has rights that a white man need respect." The chastity of my daughter cannot be protected as an American citizen, because African blood courses her veins; consequently she has " no rights that a white man need respect." She has no virtue that a white man need regard. She has no honour that a white man need admire, no noble qualities he need appreciate. The negro race is scourged beyond the beneficent range of both authorities, secular and religious. We plead their rights in the name of the immortal Declaration of Independence, and in the still more glorious name of Jesus Christ, our blessed Saviour. We beg for mercy; while the slave-whip, red with blood, cracks over them in mockery. We invoke the aid of the ambassadors of Him who came to " preach deliverance to the captives, and set at liberty them that are bound." We cry to humanity for help, but are repulsed. We appeal to American Christianity, but it refuses to shield them; to the coloured man " its bones are brass and its feathers iron."

We will turn again to the subject of our narrative. We have a different method still by which slaves escape, and none the less effectual because of its novelty. The Abolitionists in the slave States (for there are many, though they cannot advocate their principles) very kindly give the slaves information as to the direction of Canada, and the free States through which they must pass to reach it, also the names of the most important rivers, all which information the slaves remember. With this instruction alone, the slave starts for Canada; the north star is his guide, by it he knows his course. When the clouds intervene, and thus obscure the flickering light of this "beautiful star," Nature has a substitute. A smooth soft substance called moss, which grows on the bark of the trees, is thicker on the north side of the tree, and thus serves as a guide northward till the heavenly guide again appears. Necessity, it is said, is the mother of invention, which is certainly true in the case of the slave discovering such a substitute. The number of slaves who thus find their way to Canada we have no means of ascertaining, but we have reason to believe it is very great. At the birth of Jesus, the star was a guide to the wise men of the east, to Bethlehem. Over the birthplace of the "King of kings," it became stationary; in the case of the slave it is *vice versâ*—the star stops not, but the slaves does on his arrival in Canada. We realize with much pleasure "that the Lord God is a sun and a shield. He will give grace and glory, and no good thing will He withhold from them that walk uprightly." "Bow down thine ear, O Lord, and hear the poor and needy." He hears the prayer of the fugitive slave, for many are devoted Christians.

They can say with David, "Give ear, O Lord, unto my prayer, and attend to the voice of my supplications." "All nations whom Thou hast made shall come and worship before Thee." Oh, may Africa come and enjoy this privilege! May the 4,000,000 of slaves, in the United States, come: but they are legally prevented; thirty-nine lashes is the reward of each if found off his owner's premises, whether to worship God or otherwise, unless with a written consent of the owner.

It was a strange oversight on the part of the conservators of slavery, when they passed the Fugitive Bill (for law it is not), and especially when they determined upon systematic measures for its rigorous execution. In no other way could they have done so much to increase the agitation they had determined to suppress. In no other way could the public attention have been drawn to the diabolical character of slavery, and to the wickedness and meanness of its northern allies and supporters. The north, in many respects, does the bidding of the south; they are slave-hunters for their masters, the slaveholders; they are not permitted to be anything else if they obey the Fugitive Bill, and, I am sorry to say, many do. I say, they are slave-catchers for the south, as the following will show, which occurred in 1852 :—

James Phillips, a coloured man, who had lived fourteen years in Harrisburgh, Penn., much respected, and employed in a confidential situation on a railway, while on duty was suddenly surprised, knocked down, and then taken before Commissioner Richard McAllister, and in a summary manner, and by an irregular process, delivered up into slavery. I ask, in the name of humanity, who did this atrocious and abominable act?—a northern commissioner, who holds his office by the will and consent of the people. The character of the fugitive entitling him to the confidence of the people, they bought him, after he had been given up by the Commissioner. Burns was taken back from Boston, the hot-bed of abolitionism; the north gave him up.

The north supports slavery, both Church and State. But for the Underground Railroad, very few slaves would be able to reach Canada, coming, as they are compelled, through the northern States, among as rank a set of slaveholders as are to be found in South Carolina; men in the northern States who own slaves in the south; merchants in New York, Boston, Philadelphia (but especially New York), who have mortgages on slave plantations in the south. The northern churches have not sufficient courage, and still less Christianity, to open their mouths, and "plead the cause of the widow" and orphan children. Fugitives may be dragged out of their own churches and congregations, and hurried before the commissioners; and before the service of the church is concluded, their trial is over, and the poor slave is on his way to the south; yet these ministers, as a mouthpiece for God, are dumb as Balaam's ass, and, therefore, their congregations cannot be expected to be better. Notwithstanding this dark picture, there is a bright side to it; and on this side are the Beechers, the Cheevers, and many others. In some communities, the fugitive can pass 'unmolested (yet he is still liable to be betrayed even by the meanest person), but these places are few and far between; therefore we are necessitated 'to manage our affairs with great care, as the following circumstance will illustrate:—

(At one time, while in the State of Ohio, I lived near Kentucky slave State. I was rather notorious as a negro-stealer, and it was reported that I would absolutely refuse to deliver up a slave. One day a young man came to my house (I did not ask him whether he was a slave or not); he merely said he was travelling on his way to Canada. I knew, from his appearance, he was a fugitive slave, which he did not conceal. In a couple of hours his pursuers were in town, hunting for him. Before I could possibly remove him from my house, even for my own or his safety, it was literally surrounded by them. As my house was detached from any other, there was no possibility of removing him without being seen. I was at my wits' end; what to do I knew not. If the slave was caught in my possession, I must pay a fine of 1000 dollars and be imprisoned six months, neither of which was desirable, especially having a wife and children. The slave-hunters demanded my door to be opened, that they might search my house. I am not as obedient as I ought to be, even in cases where duty is at stake; therefore it is not to be wondered at that I should be so in this case. I absolutely refused to comply, unless they had authority from the mayor of the town. As they did not attempt to come in, I took it for granted that they did not possess that authority, in which con-clusion I found I was correct. This defect was met by despatching one of their company into the town or merely up the street, after a warrant. Action of some kind was imperative. In a short space of time I must submit to have my house searched. Just at this trying moment, I found the great necessity, or advantage, of having a wife. She rose from her seat, as if by Divine influence, and said, "I think it possible to save him." She immediately dressed him in her own attire, and in a few minutes he was transformed into the image of a female. Feeling myself somewhat relieved, I opened the front door, and the supposed ladies passed out. The eyes of the infuriated tigers were directed into the house, through the door, as this was the first opportunity they had had; consequently the women attracted no attention whatever, as it was a man they were in pursuit of. She took him a couple of miles in the country, and delivered him into the

charge of our conductors there. The same evening he
took a free passage to Canada. When the warrant
came, I was quite prepared for my house to be
searched, which was done. They ran to and fro, and
up and down stairs, like hungry wild beasts, dash-
ing about my chairs, sofa, &c., as though they were
iron. I spoke in a very commanding tone of voice, as
I am told I can do when a little aroused,—"Gentlemen, the law allows you, when authorized as you are,
to search my house, but not to break my furniture,
and the next man that dashes any article as that man
did" (pointing to the scoundrel) "does it at his own
risk,"—my babe (eighteen months old) crying in my
arms. This brought everything to a perfect stand-
still and dead silence: all their eyes were placed on
me, and mine were placed on them. The cries of my
child only served to augment my determination. The
child's mother being engaged in delivering the fugitive out of the power of his pursuers, and I having
undertaken the charge of the children, I must be
faithful to the trust my wife committed to me, and
faithful also to the flying slave. Eventually, one of the
men, in a kind of unnatural nasal sound, dropping his
sheepish-looking eyes on the floor, said, with feelings
of much disappointment, "Might as well go, I reckon;
no nigger here, I guess." I do not know whether
they ever discovered that he had been in my house or

D

the method of his escape; but of this I am satisfied, that they never got their victim.)

I regard the deliverance of this fugitive, by the agency of my wife, as a direct interposition of God, effectually operating through her. We are told in his Word, that " every good and perfect gift cometh down from the Father of Lights, in whom is no variableness, nor shadow of turning." This may be considered one, the evidence of which is found in the fact of its effectuality. We may well adopt the cogent language of David, " In Thee, O Lord, do I put my trust; let me never be put to confusion: deliver me in thy righteousness, and cause me to escape. De- liver me, O my God, out of the hand of the wicked: out of the hand of the unrighteous and cruel man." I hope, and verily believe, that this prayer will even- tually be answered in the behalf of 4,000,000 of slaves, in the hands of unrighteous owners, in the United States. If they should run away, doing their owners no moral injury whatever, they are hunted with dogs over mountain-tops, and through the val- leys, and shot down like deer. William Smith, who was arrested in Columbia, Pennsylvania, on his at- tempting to escape, was literally shot dead by a slave- catcher, Ridgels, of Baltimore. Who will not say these are unrighteous men? and who would like to be in their possession? A young man, named Lewis,

fled from his master in Kentucky, and came to
Cincinnati, Ohio, probably about fifty or sixty miles
from his home. Being in a free State, and among
Abolitionists, he vainly supposed himself safe. He
had left behind him a companion to whom he was
betrothed, and desirous to know whether he should
ever realize his expectations as to obtaining her, he
made application to a fortune-teller, who required
from him a synopsis of his history to begin with,
which he unhesitatingly, and in full confidence, gave
her. He left her house highly pleased with the idea
of receiving soon the object of his first love; he
almost fancied he had her in his embraces, no longer
twain, but one flesh. Time, the true test of all
things, soon taught our young friend it was all
imagination's dream, for in a few days he was
arrested as a fugitive slave. On the following morning the trial came on, in the court-house. There
was no possible chance of saving him by law, so
we made as great a noise about it as possible, to
awaken sympathy and a proper sense of justice in
the public mind. The court-house was literally filled
with white and coloured persons. Barristers were
employed on both sides. Some technical question
arose between them, and they became much excited,
questioning each other's veracity and integrity; they
rose on their feet, face to face, and each kept ap-
pealing to the judge. The people were thoroughly

excited, and their attention was wholly fixed on the
barristers and the judge. The prisoner, in charge of
the sheriff, stood near the bar, and close behind were
the people. Near the prisoner stood my friend; he
put his hat on the prisoner's head, who, taking the
hint, immediately bowed himself to the floor, and, on
his hands and knees, made his way between the legs
of the crowded assembly, and escaped, and was, in a
few minutes, out of sight. When the judge had
decided the point at issue, the sheriff found the
prisoner missing, and exclaimed hastily, "Where
is the prisoner?—where is the prisoner?" The
inquiry went throughout the court-house. The
crowd simultaneously rushed towards the door; those
who had committed themselves to negro-catching
were most eager in the search for the prisoner, for
the paltry reward offered by the owner. The more
respectable portion of the people were not very
active in looking for the prisoner, but rather, among
themselves, enjoyed the cleverness of the trick. The
sheriff, being responsible for the prisoner, offered a
reward of 1000 dollars for the recapture of Lewis,
who had escaped from the court-house. This tran-
spired on Saturday. On Sunday morning we dressed
him in female attire, and escorted him to church; we
made a collection in a quiet way, and sent him off to
Canada, where coloured men are free. It was the
fortune-teller, to whom Lewis had gone respecting

his sweetheart, and to whom he had divulged the
secret of his being a fugitive slave, that caused
him to be captured. The wretch was paid 100
dollars (£20) for the information she gave to his
owner.

(Some years ago slavery existed in Delaware, and
running away was then as much in practice as it is
now; consequently numbers of them repaired to
Philadelphia. A Mr. D. Godwin was in the habit of
buying these runaway slaves, thus: he paid the masters a small sum and took the chance of catching
them; of course, if he did not get them, he lost
his money; but if he did, the slaves were his. In
this way Mr. Godwin purchased a slave named
Ezekiel, commonly called Zeke. Mr. G. came to
Philadelphia, and called on Isaac T. Hopper, a strong
Abolitionist, for information as to the whereabouts
of this Zeke. While talking with Mr. Hopper,
up came a black man, who paid the utmost attention
to the conversation; when finished, he said, "How
do you do, Mr. Godwin? don't you know me?" He
answered that he did not. "Then you don't remember a man that lived by your neighbour, Mr. —— ?"
continued he. When he specified the time, and some
other particulars, he said he did recollect such a
person. "Well," answered the black man, "I am he,
and I am Zeke's brother." The speculator inquired
if he knew where his brother was. "Oh, yes, Mr.

Godwin, but I am sorry you have bought Zeke; you'll never make anything of him." "Why, what is the matter with Zeke?" "When such fellows as my brother come to Philadelphia, they get into bad company; they are afraid to be seen about in the day, and they go prowling about at night. I'm sorry you have bought Zeke; he is just such a character, though he is my brother." Mr. Godwin, thinking it was rather a bad case, said, "Suppose you buy Zeke?" "I should have to maintain him if I did," replied the black man. "Suppose, however, I should, what would you take for him?" The trader asked 150 dollars, which the black man most decidedly refused to give; however, he came down to sixty dollars. The black man went out, and soon returned with the money. Mr. Hopper, the Abolitionist, drew up the deed of purchase, and when duly signed the black man said, "Zeke is free!" "Yes," said Mr. Godwin. The black man, not believing the trader, turned to Mr. Hopper, the Quaker, saying, "Zeke is free, nobody can take him, can they, Mr. Hopper?" Mr. Hopper replied, "Wherever Zeke is, I assure thee, he is free." Being thus assured, the black man made a low bow towards the ground, and, with a droll expression of countenance, said, "I hope you are well, Mr. Godwin; I am happy to see you, sir. I am Zeke!" The trader seized Zeke by the collar, and began to threaten and abuse him. Zeke said, "If you don't let go, Mr. Godwin, I'll knock you down; I am a free citizen of these United States, and won't be insulted in this way by anybody." Zeke was taken before the magistrate, who, after hearing the particulars, said to Mr. Godwin, "Zeke is as free as any one in this room, and you have been out-witted."

A slave, with his wife and child, made their escape, and had spent two weeks in the forest, without anything to eat for four days, not daring to show themselves to any one, for fear of being captured, fast losing their physical strength, hunger preying upon their vitals, almost exhausted with fatigue as well, and the hope of living to reach a land of freedom having nigh fled, though an instinctive desire to do so still lingered in their careworn bosoms. In this condition seeing a gentleman, as they were concealed near his farm, passing to and fro, they ventured to show themselves, not knowing whether he was a friend or foe; alas! he was an enemy. He provided them with food as requested, in a house detached from his own dwelling; feeling assured that they were safe, they partook of their meals with great pleasure; hope began to revive, and their hearts filled with joy. But, alas! in one short hour their hopes were blasted. Joy was turned into sorrow, peace into confusion. The farmer had betrayed them; eleven men came with him to capture them. They were betrayed into the hands of wicked men; escape was out of the question. The child seemed conscious of its danger, which it manifested by screams and holding on to its mother's tattered rags. Poor woman! unable to protect herself, and no law to secure the freedom of fugitives in the United States, —the cries of the slave-mother's child went up to heaven against their oppressors. The husband placed himself at the door, but soon fell back on the floor helpless. The wife took his place, and, more successful than he, she felled three men to the ground. But, alas! resistance was vain. Overcome, she seized the knife with which she had been eating her food; resolute as death seizes his victims, intoxicated with madness—"oppression makes a wise man mad"—she placed her hand on the head of the innocent child, saying, "It was for your sake I started for Canada; I would rather see you dead than go back to slavery." So, suiting the action to the expression, she cut its throat, and immediately surrendered. Her master sold her for 1000 dollars (£200). Slavery had crushed out a mother's affection, or, may we not say it was affection that induced her to rescue the child from worse than death?

In the county of Fayette, State of Ohio, in a small village of about 1000 inhabitants, was one of our Underground Railway stations, in charge of a good and faithful conductor. Unwisely, not less than ten or twelve fugitive slaves had stopped in this town, protected only by public opinion. True, the majority of the people were Abolitionists, yet the liberty of fugitives was by no means secure. Unexpectedly, as a thief in the night, the town was invaded by four slave-holders, who, with the police, captured three of the slaves; the others contrived to make their escape into the forest. The whole town was aroused in a few minutes. The three captured slaves were in charge of one of the company, while the others were on the look-out for the fugitives who had fled to the forest. It was dangerous for us, under such circumstances, to harbour them in our houses, for fear they should be searched. There was no time to lose; what was done must be done quickly.

Sixteen of our party suddenly and furiously rushed upon the captured slaves, and cut the ropes with which their limbs were tightly bound, pushing them about from one to the other. Not a word was spoken the whole of the time it took to accomplish our design. It being warm weather, we wore slippers without heels, to prevent a noise while rescuing the prisoners and conveying them away. When we had faithfully as well as hastily performed our duty, we scampered off in different directions. It was obvious that our impetuosity had produced the effect intended on the mind of the Southerner. He was perfectly astounded and literally terrified at our unexpected approach, and

the earnestness with which we went at our work.
When a little recovered from the shock, he poured
forth a volley of oaths, threatening to shoot us if we
did not cease, to which we paid no attention whatever.   He changed his tactics by calling aloud,
"Police! police!"   These officers were intentionally
deaf, or so far off that they were unable to come to
his aid until we were quite out of sight.   Though
they pretended to be very much excited, and were
looking for us, of course they did not find our whereabouts.   We concealed the three men in a cellar,
where it was not at all likely they would be found.
The others made their escape by the assistance of
Abolitionists in the country.   When the alarm was
given in the town, and the news spread from house
to house that three slaves were captured, the others
had sufficient time to secure their liberty by ap-
pealing effectually to their legs for aid, which they
willingly gave.

.   When thus fleeing from town into the dense forest,
leaping fences, hedges, and ditches, some of their
white friends followed them closely, to baffle the
slaveholders should they follow; thus it would have
been difficult to distinguish the slaves.   These
white friends were to conduct them, when in the
forest, to a place of safety.   Our town, and even our
houses, were watched so closely, for several days,
that it was no longer safe for us or the fugitives,

that they should remain. To avoid detection, we obtained a box, about seven feet long and three feet deep, into which we put two of the men, side by side; we made holes in the sides of the box for ventilation, and thus we conveyed them eight miles to another station, where we met with their companions. The day following we took the other man in the same way, without the least suspicion, by putting the box on a wagon; when all together, they took passage on the Underground Railway to Canada.

America, professedly the freest land in the world, professes to recognize the natural and inalienable rights of all men, and, in confirmation thereof, quotes the immortal Declaration of Independence :— " We hold these truths to be self-evident, that all men are created free and equal, and are endowed, by their Creator, with certain inalienable rights, among which are life, liberty, and the pursuit of happiness." They tell us it is a fact that needs no evidence—it is a self-evident truth, founded in the very nature of man, every way congenial to the nature of things—"that all men are created free," with a free will, free mind, free use of his intellectual faculties: yet the slave cannot will himself practically free; his will is subject to the will of his master. He cannot will to have a wife, unless it is the will of his master, and should the master be willing, he has no will in living with her, and their continuing together rests entirely on the will and in-

terest of the owner.   He has no will in the education
of his children ; his intellectual powers are dormant
and stultified, his moral perceptions blunted by not
being educated.   The white man can be educated for
a lawyer or judge, a senator, a minister, a president,
&c.   The black man is educated only as a "hewer of
wood and a drawer of water."   The children of the
latter are sold to pay for the education of those of
the former, and, strange to say, they are even sold to
contribute towards evangelizing the world.   I remember seeing, during my youthful days, in the State of
South Carolina, a girl sold to contribute to a mission
in China.   Is this what the Americans mean by all
men being created free ?   Where is their equality ?
The term slave indicates inequality ; 4,000,000 are in
the prison-house of bondage this day, deprived of their
natural rights and privileges as citizens, as men, as
Christians, and as members of social and civil society.
No Bibles, no tract societies, no Bible societies, no
Sunday-school organizations, no missionary organizations, no churches nor chapels, no ministers.   This
is the rule.   Exceptions there are, I admit. Dwelling
seventeen years in the slave States enables me to know
the truth of what I state. Mothers are sold from their
children, which is a literal fact—"Rachel would not
be comforted, because they are not "—husbands from
their wives, sons from their fathers and fathers from
their sons, daughters from their mothers and mothers

from their daughters, brothers from their sisters and sisters from their brothers, and so on through the entire families of the slaves. All this is done to furnish the houses the owners live in; to build chapels, court and state houses, with their lofty spires, the finger of man's devotion, pointing heavenward; to pay the salaries of ministers, to pay the pew-rents, to buy the bread used at the Lord's table, &c. A fugitive slave told me his brother was a member of a church with him, and that his master sold him, and, to his certain knowledge, a portion of the money was spent in buying plates, which were used at the administration of the Lord's Supper. I ask, in the name of a God of justice and humanity, where is the equality of which the Americans boast so much?

A slave, feeling he has a right to his freedom, peaceably walks off in the night, in search of a country in which he may just as peaceably live and enjoy his freedom as others do. The owner may pursue and chain him beneath the shadow of Bunker Hill, or even on the grave in which lie, in silence, Washington's sleeping remains, and take him back into slavery. All this is sanctioned by the laws of the country. All this is connived at by the northern ministers and churches, and boldly declared, by the southern ministers and churches, to be a divine right, in which their northern brethren are divinely obligated to unite, and assist them in subjugating poor fugitives. Thus they make the religion of our Lord a slave-catching religion, a man-stealing and woman-whipping religion.

> " United States, your banner wears
>   Two emblems—one of Fame ;
> Alas ! the other that it bears
>   Reminds us of your shame.
> The white man's liberty in types
>   Stands blazoned by your stars ;
> But what's the meaning of your stripes ?
>   They mean your negro scars."
>
> T. CAMPBELL.

The providence of God may be obviously seen in the many successful escapes of fugitive slaves from the slave States to Canada, many of whom are pious and devoted Christians, who truly " walk by faith, and not by sight." We are now about to enter upon one of the most interesting of these narratives, to me at least, viewed in connection with Divine Providence. I may venture to tell the name of this person, Mr. Hedgman, a Christian slave in the State of Kentucky, who, for a trivial fault, was sold from a Christian wife. He did as slaves generally do in such cases, humbly, but unwillingly, submitted to his fate, and put his trust in God, praying and waiting. Too true, many of them pass from the busy scenes of this life to the world of peace without in the least degree realizing their expectations. Here is a Christian brother, for a fault not amounting to a crime, bound in cold iron chains, with the lash cracking over his innocent head. In this brother may be seen the image of God; his soul, no doubt, has been redeemed by the precious blood of Jesus. He is now to go to the cotton plantation or the sugar-field. Sorrowfully he casts a wishful look at his dear wife, the tears standing in his manly eyes; again he looks away: his mind is occupied with past recollections and fearful anticipations. Though reduced to this degradation and misery, he is calm and collected, notwithstanding he occasionally, with a sigh, gives vent to the deep-heaving of his heart, at the thought of separation, having no hope of seeing his wife again in this life. Press, dear reader (if married), thy partner to thy heart, and thank God you were both born free. His wife shared his grief—his mutual burden bore, female-like—a woman's reign is that of love—she wept aloud! At the command of the driver he moved slowly away; he stepped with much difficulty, from the weight of sorrow on his mind and chains on his body. His wife clung to him with all the strength of a woman's muscles, and anxiety of a female heart. "O my husband! my husband! my dear husband!" Alas! she was abruptly torn from his person. O Heaven, witness this parting scene! Angels, paint it on the scroll of eternity! Let Gabriel write it in the book of God's remembrance, that these guilty wretches may not escape the punishment which their sins justly merit. They tread upon ground angels would tremble to approach. "What God has joined together let no man put asunder." Outraged humanity

cries against the slaveholder. Widows and orphan
children will rise up to condemn him in the final account. It will be more tolerable for Sodom and Go-
morrah in the Judgment than for the slaveholder thus
acting. "God is not in all his thoughts." This man
travelled 1500 miles to New Orleans, and was sold
like a beast in the shambles. He prayed to God to
provide a way for his escape, and his prayer was answered, for he made his escape. He travelled night
after night, living on spontaneous productions (which
are pretty plentiful in warm climates), wading through
creeks and marshes. When going through the marshes
in the valley of the Mississippi, the alligators would
snap at him, their jaws, like two flat planks, coming
in contact with force sufficient to take off a limb; he
would leap from them in a contrary direction, crying
"Lord, have mercy upon me," and alight, perhaps,
close to another, and then leap again, praying to the
Lord for safety. He was in perils from wild beasts,
the hissing serpent was his companion, the croaking
of the owl was familiar to his ear, the howling of the
wolf, &c.; all these dangers did not make him afraid,
for he felt the protecting arm of the Lord, who sways
the universal sceptre, and holds the hearts of kings in
his hands.

Winter came on before his arrival in Canada, and
food was quite hard to get. Being some four days
without anything to eat, he was fatigued and dis-

couraged, almost exhausted, his feet frost-bitten and swollen, starvation stared him in the face,—the pelting rain from the watery clouds he was familiar with. But hunger was preying upon his constitution, stealing his strength, weakening his muscles; from pure necessity he occasionally resolved to give himself up, and tell the people he was a runaway slave. One resource yet remained, to appeal to Almighty God. In the dense forest he bowed down on a log of wood, and, in his simple and childlike manner, informed his God of his condition, saying, " O Lord ! you fed the prophet by the raven—now feed me : if you don't I shall surely die. You gave the Israelites water, and something to eat, in the wilderness—now, O God, give me something to eat." He resumed his journey, on faith of his prayer being answered. As he passed out of the wood, he discovered, in the mountains, a small cabin; he went up to it, and met with a good reception. The landlord said to him, " You are running away.; I hope you'll get along safe." This man gave him a ham and some bread, and on he went; here was an answer to his prayer. The next difficulty which he encountered was a river frozen over, with the ice not sufficiently thick to walk on, and he knew not how to cross it, for he could not swim. He stood on the banks of that river, and prayed. He asked God to deliver him from slavery and all its evils, and enable him to cross the river.

. E

When he had concluded his prayer, he got a stick and broke the ice. He then commenced fording the river, trying the depth as he proceeded; it became deeper and deeper, till it was neck-high. Providentially this was the full depth of the river, and he arrived safely on the other side. It was the cold month of January, so that the water froze on him, and he was a complete statue of ice; in this condition he first thanked God for his deliverance, and then proceeded on his journey, and eventually reached Canada. He was a man of no ordinary natural abilities, moral courage, determination of will, and physical endurance ; and, above all, a good Christian, praying man: such persons God always blesses in the way that to Him seems best. He became a deacon of a Baptist church, and a worthy one too. Now in a land of freedom (for which he was as thankful as for many other blessings), he began to pray to God to send his wife to him. In all human probability this was a hopeless thing, but nothing is impossible with God. He well remembered that "the effectual fervent prayer of a righteous man availeth much." He continued to pray year after year, but no wife came, and there was no prospect even of her coming; still he prayed. He had prayed so much for her, that it seemed impossible to cease, though all hope had vanished from his mind; her image was so indelibly stamped on his heart that he now prayed for her as by instinct. He continued in this way for twelve years, and, one Sunday morning, in the town of Amherstburgh or Malden, on Lake Erie, during service-time, the steamer from the United States to Canada arrived there. A lady came on shore, advanced immediately up the street leading from the water, and when arrived at the chapel-door, she accosted the chapel-keeper, saying, "I am a stranger here, sir." "I see you are," said he. "Where are you from?" continued he, being anxious to know her history. "I am from Virginia." "What is your name?" he asked, hoping to do her service, if she should be in search of her husband, who might be a fugitive. "Mrs. Hedgman, sir." "Hedgman! Pray, where is your husband?" She said, "I don't know: he was sold from me twelve years ago, and was sent to New Orleans. He frequently said, if he had an opportunity, he should run away; if he is anywhere here, I should like to find him." He asked her to give him a general description of her husband, which she did, with increasing hope that she should yet see him again, her face flushing as the recollection of the past rolled across her mind. The chapel-keeper said, "If your description be correct, your husband is now in this chapel." Her eyes sparkled like the north star, on a clear winter's night; much agitated, she gazed upon him with doubtful hope, wondering if he intended to deceive her. He opened the chapel-door, and in she stepped; looking earnestly down the aisle, she recognized her husband in a moment, as he was sitting on the platform, in front of the pulpit, with his face towards the door. Her paces were quick, tears flowing down her cheeks. He did not at first identify her, as she approached, but quickly, on a second look at the stranger, he traced the features of his wife, and instantly rising, he clasped her in his arms, embracing her in ecstasy of joy. To delineate this meeting is impossible; it can better be imagined than described. To add to this exciting scene, the congregation were in a flood of tears, arising from deep sympathy for their respected deacon and his beloved, long-separated wife. Is not this an answer to persevering prayer? Like her husband, the bereaved wife had supplicated for this re-union. They are now living in Canada, doing well, under the protection of Her Majesty's Government. They now walk abroad on freedom's plains, in full enjoyment of its blessings. The above is a fact, with which I am perfectly acquainted; they are now living in that land of Providence. May we not trace, in every consecutive step, that " Æthiopia shall soon stretch out her hands unto God " ?

It is sometimes the case that masters sell their own children, not always voluntarily, but circumstances at times compel them. It is no uncommon occurrence for the master to select one of the slave women and call her his wife. The slave laws recognize no legal marriages between the negro and white races, whether bond or free. Some of the wealthy planters, no doubt, treat these adopted women with as much kindness and care as the iniquitous law will allow. Such was the case with a slaveholder in the State of Georgia, and he soon became a father, and the slave wife a mother; this united them more closely in the bond of social affection, which lies at the foundation of social society. Their dear little child (a girl) increased in beauty as she advanced in age: unfortunately the mother died when the child was quite young. The father was a humane man: though a slaveholder, he was not a trader in slaves. The mother was a quadroon, and the father a white man, therefore there was no appearance of African blood coursing the veins of the lovely child, of whom the father thought so much. He sustained double relationship to this child, both as father and master; but for this the child would have been a precious jewel in social society. The thought of being a slave never once entered her bosom to ripple the peaceful stream of pleasure in her onward journey of life. As she ripened into womanhood, her kind father educated her in his own house; though contrary to law, this infringement was tolerated through the influential position of the father in the community. At a proper age she became the mistress of his house, which, to some extent, precluded the necessity for his marrying, which had he done, the child's condition might have been made known to herself and others. Eventually, this planter failed in business, and then came hard times for his poor daughter, whose name was Mary. The farm and all the field-hands, with other property, were taken to satisfy his creditors. His legal adviser balanced his accounts, and found the planter still minus 1000 dollars (£200). He asked the planter if he had given in all the property he could spare, and he answered him in the affirmative. The lawyer, running his accustomed eyes down the list of property, consisting of land, horses, cows, hogs, wagons, ploughs, and human beings, in one common class, said, " I don't see your housemaid's name here." He touched a tender chord in the father's heart, which vibrated and shocked his very soul. He was not aware his adviser knew anything of his relationship to her as a master; he said, " She is my daughter." " True," replied the former, " but she is your slave as well. She is worth 1000 dollars of any man's money; if you are willing, I will give that for her, and then you will be entirely out of debt." He persistingly and most decidedly refused. The adviser, knowing the embarrassed circumstances of the planter, continued to urge a consent to his proposition, and said, " We shall be under the dis-

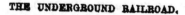

agreeable necessity of having her seized by the sheriff, and sold on the auction-block to the highest bidder; it is, therefore, much better, both for you and her, to make a private sale." His daughter was in the power of the law, and he in the power of his creditors; with the greatest reluctance, he submitted to the proposition, and sold his own dear child. Justice cries against this horrible deed. Outraged humanity lifts her powerless voice, and weeps aloud. Mercy pleads in vain the fate of this helpless young woman, fixed by law, because she was a slave, her mother being one; and the children follow the condition of the mother.

That this is the practice, sanctioned by law, in the finest country in the world, the following will show. " Out of thine own mouth will I judge thee."

LOUISIANA.—" That slaves shall always be reputed and considered real estate: shall, as such, be subject to be mortgaged, according to the rules prescribed by law; and they shall be seized and sold as real estate."

MARYLAND.—" In case the personal property of a ward shall consist of specific articles, such as slaves, working beasts, animals of any kind, stock, furniture, plate, books, and so forth, the court, if it shall deem it advantageous to the ward, may, at any time, pass an order *for the sale thereof.*"—Chap. C. No. 12.

The notorious Henry Clay, in the United States'

Senate, in 1839, based his argument against the abolition of slavery on the value of the slaves as *property*. The following is his language :—

"The third impediment to immediate abolition is
to be found in the immense amount of capital which
is invested in slave property." The total value of
slave property then, by estimation, was twelve hundred millions of dollars. "And it is rashly proposed,
by a single fiat of legislation, to annihilate this immense amount of *property* without *indemnity*, and
without compensation to the owners,—that is, property, which the law declares to be property. Two
hundred years of legislation have sanctified and sanctioned negro slaves as property." It follows that slave-
holding is identified with chattelhood. In this argument the slaveholders confide; the nation consents,
and, therefore, slavery exists with all its evils. One of
the sublime lessons of Christianity teaches the slaveholder to "do unto others as he would have others do
unto him." He never dreams that the degraded slave
is within the pale of this holy canon. For two hundred
years has legislation endeavoured to sanctify or purify
slavery. Legal is not always moral, therefore legislative assent can never rectify a moral wrong. "Cease
to do evil, and it shall go well with thee." We may
justify polygamy on the same principle. An African
king has a hundred wives; shall we count that right
because it has been legal in his dominions for two

hundred years? No legislative enactments are paramount to the holy laws of God, which He gave to Israel from the lofty summit of Mount Sinai, in the midst of thunder, storm, fire, and smoke. "He that stealeth a man and selleth him, or if he be found in his hand, he shall be put to death." This legislative act is still more ancient and binding than any that man is capable of enacting.

The young woman under consideration was property, and sold as such. The father was at a loss as to the best way of breaking to his daughter the dreadful fact that she was a slave, and that he had been obliged to sell her, and that, in a few days, she must be delivered to her purchaser. Prostrated before the altar of degradation, she must become a victim to his brutal passions, for which she was purchased. The father was unusually depressed, so much so as to amount to perfect melancholy, and occasionally much agitated. This was observed by poor Mary, who attributed it to the embarrassment he was in. All of a sudden, he called out "Mary!" "Well, papa," was her reply, her dark eyes looking in his, with a cheering smile, little dreaming what was about to fall from the lips of him in whom she had placed implicit confidence. "It is my heart-rending duty to tell you that you are a slave." With astonishment, as though it could not possibly be true, she gazed upon him. "O papa! you don't mean to say that I am a slave?" "Yes" (much agitated), "and, alas! you are sold." The horrors of slavery, as a mighty avalanche, rolled in upon her soul, and she fell, unconscious, to the ground.

On recovering her consciousness, as there was no time to be lost, to save herself from degradation, she obtained an interview with a gentleman of respectability and influence, to whom, unknown to her father, she was betrothed.

On his entering the room, she fell prostrate at his feet, pouring forth a flood of tears; then, with uplifted hands, her tearful eyes fixed on his, with that plaintiveness of voice of which woman only is capable, exclaimed, "Sir, I am a slave, and my father has sold me! You are the only person in this world that can save me; upon you my future welfare and happiness depend. Will you save me? What shall I hear—oh, what shall I hear from one I love so dear?" This, to him, was like a thunderbolt,—astounded, he gazed upon her in her prostrate condition (he could hardly realize that it was the object of his affections —but it was). He took her by the hands, and raised her from that position, with all the sympathy and tender feeling of which his sympathizing nature was capable. He wiped the tears from her youthful and lovely cheeks, and said, "I will save you." Weak and feeble from the shock her nervous system had undergone, she sobbed, sighed, wept, and groaned.

Measures were immediately taken to leave that land of blood. It was not a matter of choice, but stern necessity,—they flew, and came to the city of Cincinnati, in the State of Ohio, a distance of six hundred miles, where I then lived. They were immediately married, — then were their desires realized, though not under the most favourable circumstances.

As soon as her purchaser learned the fact of her successful escape, he started men, in haste, to pursue her, who tracked her even into the city where she was. The Abolitionists gave her instant notice of their presence, and she immediately left for Canada. Touching that land, sacred to freedom, her soul, like the eagle unfettered, walked abroad in its own majesty, on the flowery plains of liberty, fearless of chains. Though as white as an English lady, though legally married to a white gentleman, whose rights and privileges the Americans profess to acknowledge and protect, yet, so long as she remained in any part of the Union, she was liable to be torn from her husband's embraces, and would be, if her pursuers could ascertain her whereabouts. He might, but for the circumstances that caused their flight, have lived with her illegally in the slave State, but could not live with her legally in a free State, because she was a slave, and, under the Fugitive Bill, might be handcuffed in her own dwelling, and driven away, like an ox to the slaughterhouse. She now lives in Toronto, C. W., and I have the pleasure of her acquaintance.

Thomas Brown was arrested in Philadelphia, and rendered up to the slave-claimants. The northern judges are guilty of turning fugitives into the dark dungeon of slavery, for they could free every slave that comes before them, if so disposed, by declaring the Fugitive Bill unconstitutional, and refusing to comply with its requirements. The following will show that our railroad is doing good business, and therefore ought to be patronized, as we believe it will be :—— "Five slaves left Mr. C. D. Armstrong, of St. Louis —a girl, 18 years of age, a woman, 25, and children, supposed to have been abducted by two white men." They consider a girl at 18 years of age not a woman, as may be inferred from the above distinction, which is quite consonant with southern custom. Generally, they call the males boys until they are about 60, after that period " old uncle," until the day of their death ; the females, gal or girl, or, sometimes, ironically, " my lady," until they are sixty, then " old aunty," to the end of life. The northern men have borrowed this custom from the southern, and presume to call free coloured men boys in the north, as the following will obviously show :—A fugitive slave, on his way to Canada, being in a free State, and so far from his home, thought himself out of danger; he ventured to take the train, as he had a little money, to travel publicly to Canada. After getting into the carriage (in the United States called car), the conductor said, "It is against our rules for coloured men to go first-class." The fugitive was of a light complexion,—he said, "Am I coloured? Look at me." The conductor, supposing it possible he might only be a dark-skinned man, begged his pardon, and left him. He afterwards took another view of him, and, not being satisfied on the point, called the second conductor, and asked him if he did not think the man in question a nigger. He said, "Certainly he is." They violently dragged him out, although he had a first-class ticket. He got on the freight carriage. Nearing their destination, the same conductor, collecting fares and gathering tickets, came to the fugitive: "I say, boy." The fugitive seemed to be deaf. "Boy, I say,—I mean you,—ticket, ticket." The fugitive said, "What do you charge per hundred for freight?" The conductor replied, "25 cents." "I weigh just 150 lbs.; as I am freight and not a passenger, I will pay you accordingly;" which he did.

The Abolitionists are continually accused of exaggerating the cruelties inflicted upon the slaves. It is said, they are "well off." In the language of a senator, many of them are "fat and sleek." "They are, generally, not overtasked; they are content, merry, fond of singing and sports; in better condition than the free people in the north, or operatives besides, they are protected by public sentiment in their several localities, in opposition to the Fugitive Bill, which is unparalleled in the jurisprudence of nations. Where individual liberty is only secured by public sentiment, though that sentiment may be, and sometimes is, better than the law, yet freedom under such circumstances is never safe and secure. This sentiment must, when occasion requires, yield to the rigorous demands of the law, however unjust they may be. To insure the permanent security of human freedom, we must have the sanction of law combined with public sentiment, from which law emanates. The legislatures of some States, though few, have declared the nefarious Fugitive Bill unconstitutional, and have refused the use of their prisons for the security of the slaves when arrested. This renders it more difficult to capture them, but even with these obstructions many are captured in those States. In confirmation of the assertion relative to the insecurity of escaped slaves in the free States, I adduce the first part of the sixth section of the Fugitive Bill:—

"And be it further enacted, that when a person held to service or labour in any State or territory of the United States has heretofore, or shall hereafter, escape into another State or territory of the United States, the person or persons to whom such service or labour may be due, or his, her, or their agent or

attorney duly ████████. ███ ████
writing, acknowledge a ████ ███ ████
some legal officer of ██
in which the ███ █ █ ████
and reclaim such ████ █ ███ ██ ██
ing a warrant from a ████
commissioners appoint__ ██ ██
trict, or county, for the apprehend
from service or labour; or by ████ ████
fugitive, where the same can be ██ ██
and by taking and causing such per-
forthwith before such court, jud__ or ████████
whose duty it shall be to hear a ██ ██████
case of such claimant in a summary manner

Should the fugitive endeavour to ██ ██
the free States he may be pursue_ ██ ██
attempt to evade the hunter, and for those ██
tory of the United States he is st__ ██
taken in therefore it flows he is now in ██
him Republic such fugitive, we ██ ██
arrested without first obtaining a warrant ██
court, judge, or commissioner, without ██ ██
ping the bounds of legal authority. He is ██
forthwith before such tribunal as are mentioned, giving the criminal or culprit ██
extricate himself

Still adding insult to injury, the case is ██
and determined in a "summary manner" ██

in England, and would not leave their masters if they could." What we have said already is quite sufficient to disprove that. Mrs. Stowe is accused of misrepresenting the matter in "Uncle Tom's Cabin." There being 45,000 fugitive slaves in Canada, does not seem to indicate that they were very well treated, otherwise they would have remained in that professedly happy condition. We suppose, having no means of ascertaining the precise facts of the case, that of the present generation of slaves, 90,000 have attempted to secure their freedom by running away, but only 45,000 have succeeded. The advertisements for runaways, with which the southern papers are crowded, demonstrate the discontent of the slaves, and their longings for freedom. The unwillingness of the slaveholders to bring their slaves to the north, during their summer pilgrimages, testifies their apprehensions on the subject. Happy, indeed! Who can describe the sufferings of parents for ever bereft of their children; mothers robbed of their daughters; children torn from their parents; young women, and married women, exposed to the brutal lusts of slave-drivers, masters, and overseers; millions doomed to insult, deprived of opportunities to read God's word, to attend upon his worship, to instruct their children; and taunted for their religious principles? Advocates for slavery, would you be happy under such circumstances? Certainly not; then think not

that others can be. The day of judgment only will
disclose those registered wrongs of which the coloured
men, women and children are the victims in the slave
States.

The facts I narrate of the sorrows of the down-
trodden negroes may be considered exaggerations by
the ignorant and unfeeling; but surely not by the
recording angel, who drops a tear at every record
made. Nor can they be by the compassionate Saviour,
who tells their wanderings, puts their tears into his
bottle, and writes them in his book of remembrance.

The following letter is from the *New York Daily
Times*, written by a person who visited the Dismal
Swamps, the celebrity of which has gone far and wide
as the habitation for runaway slaves :—

"The Dismal Swamps are noted places of refuge
for runaway negroes. They were formerly peopled in
this way much more than at present; a systematic
hunting of them, with dogs and guns, having been
made by individuals who took it up as a business,
about ten years ago, has caused these swamps to be
less frequented. Formerly, children were born, bred,
lived, and died there. The negro, my guide, told me he
had seen skeletons there, and had helped to bury bodies
recently dead. There are people in the swamps now,
he thought, that are children of fugitives, and fugitives themselves finish their lives there. What a
strange life it must be! He said, the drivers some-

times shoot them. When they saw a fugitive, if he tried to run away from them, they would call out to him, and, if he did not stop, they would shoot the poor fellow, and sometimes killed him. 'But some of them would rather be shot than taken, sir,' he added simply. . . . . No particular breed of dogs is used for hunting the negroes. Bloodhounds, fox-hounds, bulldogs, and curs were used. A white man told me how they trained them for the work, as though it was a common and notorious practice. They are shut up when puppies, and never allowed to see a negro except while training to catch him. A negro is made to run from them, and they are encouraged to follow him, until he gets into a tree, when they are given meat; after which they teach them to follow any particular negro by scent. A shoe, or piece of cloth-ing, is taken off a negro, and the dogs are taught to scent out the owner of it, and to tree him. When the drivers take a negro that has not a pass or free paper, and they don't know whose slave he is, they confine him in gaol, and advertise him. If no one claims him within a year, he is sold to the highest bidder, at a public sale."

I quite understand the method of training dogs, as I have seen it many times. Sometimes they drag a child on the ground, holding the puppy's nose to the place until he follows voluntarily. Occasionally they suffer the dog to bite it a little so as to taste the blood, and thus make it vicious. Slavery is, as the venerable John Wesley said, "the sum of all villanies."

It is absurd to talk of the contentment of the slaves. Even if they were contented, slavery would still be a crime; to make a human being property is wrong—*malum in se*.

The slaves are fond of mirth and singing! So they are, but by this they only prove they are men. But it is not always an evidence of a contented and happy mind. The prisoner, under the dread sentence of death, drags his chains across the dark and gloomy dungeon, hanging to his ankles, waiting his execution, humming some favourite tune to dissipate the awful realities of eternity from his much agitated mind. None would for a moment say he had rather be a prisoner than a free man. The same rule holds good with the slave. If not, it only shows, very conspicuously, the wickedness of such a system, thus, like a crucible, crushing out of man the very element that constitutes him man, and reducing him to a beast, with only carnal appetites to gratify.

No man, whatever his complexion or condition may be, can love slavery; if he says he does, he gives the strongest possible evidence of his extreme imbecility, and ignorance of human nature. The love of liberty is an innate principle of man's mental nature, altogether beyond his control. Anything

F

that opposes the aspirations of the human mind, and
the development of man's moral nature, he hates and
opposes from the depth of his soul; slavery does this,
therefore he hates it. Some slaves are satisfied in
their condition, and would not accept their freedom.
Such I have seen and known,—but it is the exception,
not the rule. The cause of their contentment is
found in the humanity of their claimants, to whom
they are attached by their repeated kindnesses to
them. Thus it is the owners they are attached to,
and not the diabolical system, as the following will
evidently demonstrate. The notorious and far-famed
Henry Clay (the firm advocate of human chattelhood) took with him into the north, and into Canada,
his domestic servant, Bill; he defied the Abolitionists
to take him away from him. He offered to give his
servant his emancipation papers the moment he con-
sented to leave him and remain in the north, or in
Canada. Bill would not accept the overtures of the
Abolitionists; he sternly resisted them all, and declared he had rather be with his master than be free,
so he went with him to the south. Eventually, by a
stroke of Providence, Mr. Clay was brought to a sick-
bed, and death seemed inevitable. Bill knew he would
be sold with other slaves, at the death of his master,
and what hands he should get into he could not judge,
whether a Legree or a Haley; he thought it therefore
not wise to wait the death of his master, and took

a free passage to Canada, where he could be his own master. I think, if left to their own choice, this would be the result with a majority of the exceptions before referred to: this evidently shows it is the owners they are attached to, and not the system. Allow me, kind reader, to answer another objection of the opponents to emancipation. "The lives of the owners would be in danger. They would wake up* some morning and find all their throats cut." This absurdity finds no parallel in the annals of history. It assumes that the African, or slave, when treated justly, will exhibit a vindictive spirit, which he does not when treated unjustly; that when elevated to the blessings of freedom, he will thirst for human blood, which he does not do when crushed and cursed by slavery; or, if so, it is merely to obtain his pristine liberty. At present, he witnesses continually his wife torn from his arms; sees his infants brought to the auction-block; the heavenly gate of knowledge shut against him; the fruit of his hard labour unjustly taken by another; sees himself, and offspring, doomed to a wretched servitude, from which there is no redemption, all of which he quietly submits to, and patiently endures. Yet, for one single act of kindness to him and his children (a kindness for which they have prayed, and enduringly waited the answer of that prayer), now that they have obtained that desire,

* Rather difficult to wake up after their throats are cut !

they will cut the throats of the donors. It is pre-
posterous in the extreme.

I will now refer to a noble example, which glitters
in the historic page, relative to this matter. By one
single Act of Parliament, the slaves of the British
West Indies were suddenly, as well as peaceably,
changed into free men and women : their souls walked
abroad on the plains of freedom, in their own majesty,
fearless of lash or chains. The British slaves num-
bered 800,000, according to Mr. W. Goodell and the
Honourable Charles Sumner's report on the subject.
The whites and blacks, or negroes, were in the following proportion : 131,000 Whites, distributed as
follows :—In the island of Jamaica (the largest at
present), 400,000 Africans, and 37,000 whites; Bar-
badoes, 120,000 Africans, and 15,000 whites; in St.
Lucia, 19,500 Africans, and 600 whites; in Tobago,
14,000 Africans and only 600 whites; in Monserrat,
600 Africans, and only 150 whites. In all these
places no man was ever put to death by the liberated
slaves. On the contrary, the authorities positively
declare that emancipation took place in the most
peaceable manner.

Sir Lionel Smith, the Governor of Jamaica, in his
speech to the Assembly, says, their "conduct proves
how well they deserved the boon of freedom." Her
Majesty once declared from the throne, "that emancipation had taken place without any disturbance of

public order or tranquillity." I believe in the doctrine that our safety consists in doing our duty both to God and man.

We will return to our subject. In the slave States it is customary for the free coloured men to marry slave women. There is no legal marriage when one party is a slave, whether the free party be white or coloured. A free coloured man wished to purchase his wife's freedom; not having the money, he agreed with her master to work seven years for her, at the end of which he was to possess her. The man faithfully performed his duty, but at the expiration of the seven years the master refused to give her up. The oath of a coloured person being invalidated in any case where a white person is a party concerned, the man had no legal redress. The master, nevertheless, gained the confidence of the man by affirming, with all the solemnity of an oath, that he would let him have her at the end of the second seven years. The man, accordingly, served another seven years, and again the master refused to give possession of the woman. The man did then what he should have done at first; he stole her away, and three others, and started off to Canada. Being fifty miles towards the interior of the State, they proceeded direct to the Ohio river. They were pursued, and their savage pursuers reached the usual place of crossing before the fugitives, and, there lying in ambush, waited their arrival. The fugitives reached the spot in the silent hour of the night. A skiff being fastened to the bank, they hastily got into it; but, when receding from the shore, their pursuers made their appearance, and furiously plunged into the water, waist deep, and violently seized hold of the boat, determined they should not proceed, but the man holding the skiff was immediately shot dead by one of the fugitives. They then proceeded, as quickly as possible, across the river, leaving their infuriated pursuers without the means of following them. On reaching the other side of the river, they landed in the free State of Ohio, and there soon found friends to assist them on their perilous journey to a blessed land of liberty. I leave the reader to make his own comments, and to come to his own conclusions, upon the act of the fugitive taking the life of the man-stealer. It was the husband who shot the man, and thus secured the freedom of his wife and the other slaves that accompanied them. These fugitives were brought to my house, and I passed them on to Canada, where the patriarchal custom of buying wives, and paying for them by bond labour, is not the practice; that labour is required to support their wives after they have obtained them.

"Jacob served seven years for Rachel, and they seemed unto him but a few days, for the love he had for her." "He served Laban yet seven other years, and he gave him Rachel to wife." This man was by no means as good as Laban; the latter gave Jacob his wife at the termination of fourteen years, but the former refused thus to do. He cheated the man not only out of his service, but out of his wife as well. Slavery stops not here; it takes even the children from the mother; she, legally, has no children; they are her master's property.

A slave "can do nothing, possess nothing, nor acquire anything; all belongs to his master." A slave woman, in the State of Georgia, was forced to leave her child, when only six weeks old, to accompany her young mistress to the north, on a pleasure-trip. The mistress stopped in New York, but the servant continued her journey a little further north than her mistress anticipated. She arrived safe in Canada. This woman worked hard, saved what money she could for two years, and then wrote to her late master, and asked him what he would take for her child. His answer was £50. She forwarded the money to him, through an agent, and he sent the child to her. This child was not legally hers, but her master's, therefore she must purchase it from him before she could own it. Slavery steals from mothers' arms their dear ones, and leaves them to mourn their loss. The slave laws are not obsolete, as some would have you believe, but strictly conformed to, when the interest of the owner requires it. Another case, just in point, is that of Mrs. Forester, of Washington City, the capital of the

United States, who sold one of her slaves his liberty
for three hundred dollars; but his wife and three children remained her property, as he was unable to purchase them. The man paid the mistress ten dollars
per month for his wife to live with him; thus he literally hired his wife. The children lived with their
parents, so that the woman to whom they belonged
was not at the expense of feeding and clothing them.
As they grew up, and arrived at the age of ten or
twelve, the mistress had them fetched away and sold
on the auction-block to the highest bidder. Finally,
she sent the police for Benjamin, the youngest and
the only child left. Some kind friend concealed the
child, quite unknown to the parents; so that they
could not deliver him into the mistress's possession,
as the others had been. The poor man was therefore
put into prison, on the charge of concealing a runaway
slave. He was fined one hundred dollars and costs,
which amounted together to nearly two hundred dollars. He was kept in prison twelve months. He
could well adopt the cogent language of Jacob, "Jo-
seph is not, Simeon is not, and ye will take Benjamin
away: all these things are against me." The industrious habits of this slave had won for him the sympathies of the community, who voluntarily made up
the money, and paid the fine, and would, had it been
possible, have released him from his unjust imprisonment. The boy Benjamin was hurried away, with

something like lightning speed, towards the north star, and was soon beyond the possibility of recovery.

John G. Whittier, the American poet, as with a live coal dropped from freedom's altar, firing up his soul and enlivening his imagination, thus describes woman's condition in slavery :—

"What, oh ! our countrymen in chains !
    The whip on woman's shrinking flesh ;
Our soil yet reddening with the stains,
    Caught from her scourging, warm and fresh.
What ! mothers from their children riven !
    What ! God's own image bought and sold !
Americans to market driven,
    And bartered, as the brute, for gold !
Speak ! shall their agony of prayer
    Come thrilling to our hearts in vain ?
To us, whose fathers scorn'd to bear
    The paltry menace of a chain ;
To us, whose boast is loud and long,
    Of holy liberty and light ;
Say, shall these writhing slaves of wrong
    Plead vainly for their plunder'd rights ?"

To secure individual aid, they offer money, as the following will show :—In the counties of Mason and Bracken, Kentucky, an association is formed to assist in pursuing and recovering fugitives. Quite liberal rewards are offered to citizens in the free States, to help them, and many do. Four coloured citizens of Massachusetts were arrested in Galveston, Texas, for concealing a fugitive slave on board the brig 'Billow,' of Boston, with intention of aiding him in his escape. They were tried and convicted, and had to pay a fine equal to the value of the slave; in default, they were sold as slaves. The governor of the State was authorized by the legislature to take steps for their release. I do not know whether they ever were set free; but, if they had been white men, no pains, money, or time would have been spared by the State.

The following I quote from the *San Francisco Herald*, 1854.—"FUGITIVE SLAVE CASE. — Justice Shepherd issued a warrant for the arrest of a mulatto woman, who was claimed as a fugitive from labour by T. T. Smith, of Jackson County, Missouri. She was brought to this country by the claimant in 1850, and remained, together with a number of other slaves, in his family, until a few months since, when she married a free negro, and escaped. Her owner heard of her arrival here, and came down in search. Being informed that she was secreted on board the ship 'Flying Cloud,' he applied for a warrant, by virtue of which she was arrested, and brought before Justice Shepherd, by whom, on satisfactory proof of title, she was remanded to the custody of Mr. Smith, to be conveyed to the State of Missouri." Poor woman, she must go back into the dungeon of slavery, and suffer the fury of a task-master. She was not so fortunate as the fugitives whose narrative I will give next.

Before the passing of the pernicious slave law, eight fugitives travelled some two hundred miles

through the State of Ohio, to Cleveland, on the edge
of Lake Erie, from whence they must cross the lake
to reach Canada, and this they could only do on a
steamboat, and one happened to be just about ready
to start. The captain was one of the conductors of
our railroad. These eight fugitives went on board;
as they stepped on the captain turned his back to
them, so that he might be justified in saying he did
not see them come on board, if he should be questioned about them; however, they were packed away
as freight. Their pursuers were close on them.
Just before the steamer left the shore they went on
board, but they did not know their slaves were there.
They intended to go to Detroit, on the State side,
where, in all probability, they would meet them in
the act of crossing the Detroit river, going into
Canada, as they had, in their opinion, gone another
way. The next morning, about eight o'clock, the
passengers all prepared for breakfast, as the steamer
had not then arrived. These negro-catchers, walking
the deck, enjoying a morning's breeze, discovered,
unexpectedly, their negroes, packed away very snugly
all together. They passed many compliments, and
made many inquiries relative to their escape, &c.,
directing their remarks chiefly to Jack, a kind of
prince among them. Next they inquired of the
captain as to his landing-point, and the time, anxious
to secure their property. The captain said he should

be compelled to stop at Malden, *alias* Amherstburgh, on the Canada side, at the mouth of the Detroit river, still twenty miles from Detroit city, on the State side, their place of destination. Malden was the captain's place to take in wood, to enable him to run his vessel the twenty miles to Detroit.

Knowing, as they did, the moment the steamer landed at Malden the fugitives were as free as themselves, because it is British soil, they implored the captain not to stop there, for their negroes would escape. He said he had nothing to do with the negroes; it was wood he wanted, otherwise the steamer could not run. "For God's sake, captain, don't stop at Malden." "No use, gentlemen, we must have wood, or we shall be lost." "Captain, land at Detroit before you do at Malden, and we will give you three hundred dollars" (or £60). To this the captain agreed. They immediately paid him the money, and accordingly they landed at Detroit. One of these slave-catchers hastened immediately up town to obtain a warrant to arrest the fugitives, while the others stood at the gangway to see if the slaves came on shore in common with the passengers. In the meanwhile the captain gave the lookers-out (Abolitionists) to understand what was afloat. They took a yawl on the opposite side of the steamer, and pitched the fugitives into it as though they were barrels of flour. On the opposite side of the river is Canada.

The slaves rowed for their liberty, their eyes set on freedom's land, which once reached, they were safe, beneath British rule; they were filled both with joy and fear;—the approaching enemy behind them, and a land of liberty before them. The absentee returned with the sheriff, looking this way and that way, his companions being unable to give any information as to the whereabouts of the slaves, though others might, had they been so disposed. When the slaves were halfway across the river, fully out of danger, some gentlemen shouted out, "Are those your niggers? I could have told you where they were before, had I known they were yours." The slaveholder was very angry indeed. The captain very quietly informed him he had been paid the money to land there, which he had done according to contract, but he did not understand that he was to hold the negroes and keep them from walking off as other gentlemen. While the altercation was going on a gentlemen said to the Southerner, "They are not over yet, we may overtake them; for seventy-five dollars (or £15) I will do all I can in assisting you." The money was paid as before; they got into a yawl, across they went, but the fugitives arrived long before they did. They overtook them, as the gentleman said, but it was in Canada. The Southerner, knowing where he was, began to persuade Jack, the leader, by saying, "You know the old man was just as good to you as to one of his own sons; come, Jack, go back now. He has made his will since you have come away, and he says at his death he will set you all free. The old man is very sorry you have all left him." The latter, I believe, had lost eight thousand dollars. I should be quite sorry to meet such a loss. Jack had not spoken, to our knowledge, from his first discovery to this time; he very attentively listened to all the slave-holder had to say. "Well, I had a hard time getting here—I believe I will stay here now," replied Jack. The owner lost both his slaves and his money. I do not justify for a moment the manner in which he lost his money; but I certainly do justify the slaves for remaining in Canada.

I may be allowed to examine what the scriptural idea is respecting runaway slaves or fugitives for liberty. The Jews never sent after a runaway; there are cases of going after an ox or an ass, but no instance of a master going or sending after a stray servant. If the possibility of property in man had been admitted; if servants had been regarded as slaves, and masters as owners, then the laws of God would no more have permitted any two-legged property to run away from the owner, to steal itself from the master, than four-legged property a man would have had no more right to run away than a horse or an ox. The right to possess property gives a right to secure that property and prevent its escape.

If thou meet even thine enemy's ox or his ass

going astray, thou shalt surely bring it back to him again." But, "Thou shalt not deliver unto his master the servant which has escaped from his master; he shall dwell with thee, even among you, in that place he shall choose in any of thy gates where it liketh him best, but thou shalt not oppress him." In one case the Jew was quite justifiable in turning the strayed back; in the other he was not justified so to do, because the right of property was recognized in the beast, but not in man; for "in the image of God created He him." Man coming from the plastic hand of Omnipotence, with a mind capable of comprehending the nature and character of his Creator, a heart to feel, a soul to love Christ and his holy religion, and created a little lower than the angels, to be hunted down and dragged into perpetual bondage in a land calling itself free, the freest in the world, is almost incredible; but it is a lamentable fact,—a fact not to be disguised or varnished. Stealing men was a capital offence for which the offender was put to death. "He that stealeth, or selleth, or holdeth a man, shall surely be put to death."

God has thundered forth his mighty voice, as "the voice of many waters," against this wicked traffic.

"For three transgressions of Israel, and for four, I will not turn away the punishment thereof, because they sold the righteous for silver and the poor for a pair of shoes" (Amos ii. 6). God's retributive justice will not always remain silent, but erelong will be manifested in behalf of multiplied thousands of his redeemed children, sold for silver and gold, even by professed Christians. They are like the condemned miserable wretches alluded to by the Prophet, "The oppressors of God's sheep, the destroyers of men; whose possessors slay them and hold themselves not guilty; and they that sell them say, Blessed be the Lord, for I am rich." Many of the American slaveholders are rich at the expense of the blood, bones, and muscles of the slaves. The slaveholders plead divine authority for capturing fugitive slaves from the case of Hagar. No two things are more opposite than these. Hagar was a wife by the consent of Sarah, whose influence was supreme over her as well as Abraham, and Abraham sent her away, therefore she did not run away: if she had been a slave this would have freed her—instead of selling her child he gave it to her: many slaveholders sell their own children by their slave women. He also furnished her with something for her and the child to eat in their perambulations. Instead of preventing her flight, he assisted her by laying the youth, as well as the bread and water, on her shoulders. That she was a domestic servant we don't deny. She was privileged to go where she liked, so far as Abraham was concerned. If the slaveholders would act upon this principle, slavery would soon be abolished by the exit of the slaves, until such exit would become altogether unnecessary. They again assure us Paul sent back Onesimus, a slave, to Philemon, a slaveholder.—1st. It is for them to prove Onesimus was a slave. It is one thing to make an assertion, and quite another to prove it. Many persons don't like to take things for granted.—2. Having assumed so much, they must show that Philemon was a slaveholder. To many it would no doubt seem, to prove the former would be to demonstrate the latter, but it does not necessarily follow. This they have not done, for the reason—they can't. But the accumulated evidence from the passage is on the side of freedom. This eminent Apostle says, "Whom I would have retained." It seems he had power to keep him had he been disposed; from whence did he derive this power? "Thou shalt not turn back the servant that escapeth unto thee," &c. By this law Paul could have retained him; he says to Philemon, "Receive him as ye would me," not as a servant, but above a servant, a brother beloved in the Lord. Whatever might have been his previous condition, his state was now evidently that of freedom; it is quite obvious he was not a slave. Our opinion holds good till the slaveholder proves that he was. They have had two hundred years to bring forward their evidence: their failure cannot therefore be for the want of time. Jesus says, "Love the Lord thy God with all thy heart, soul, mind, strength, and thy neighbour as thyself." Paul was a consistent Christian, he could not therefore send Onesimus into slavery where he would not like to be sent himself. Again, he would in this be violating the law of love, "Do unto all men as you would they should do unto you." Paul, I am sure, would not have liked Onesimus to send him into bondage. Dragging fugitive slaves into slavery finds no shelter in the Word of God ; it is therefore a crime, and they that do it are criminals, and will be judged, convicted, and punished accordingly.

Slaves have a consciousness of right and wrong, and understand their duties as servants as well as their masters ; many will not, therefore, submit to the lash; such prefer a change of masters, though by this change their tasks may be augmented and their labour much more severe than formerly. One of this class lived in the State of Kentucky in 1846, when he made his exit to Canada; the master who sold him came to the cabin in which he lived with his aged mother, in company with his new purchaser, with a hoe and a rope in his hand, intending to knock him down and tie him, and in this condition deliver him to his new master. As the slave passed out at the door of the cabin, the stranger struck at him; the slave evaded the well-directed blow, and with his knife

stabbed the man to death. The master, endeavouring to rescue the stranger, was also killed. The
slave escaped on the best horse his master had to the
Ohio river the same night, a distance of fifty miles;
on his arrival he crossed the river in a yawl, and with
the bridle in his hand he travelled all day inquiring
for a stray horse, until the Abolitionists took charge
of him and brought him to my house on his way to
Canada. I think, however, the slave would have been
more justifiable in running away with the horse, without killing the man; perhaps he would have been
without blame had he left the horse; it was, however,
property stealing property. There are few such men
as the above, who have in this way made manifest
their capabilities of leading their brethren out of the
prison-house of bondage; that there are such, none
deny. The slaveholders themselves are aware of the
capabilities of the slaves to free themselves, if they
only knew their own power; hence come unrighteous
laws, preventing instruction—"knowledge is power."
Give the bondsman this power, and he is no longer a
vassal. Mr. H. B. left his master in Kentucky, and
found a recognition of human rights in Canada, leaving a wife and one child in slavery. Though free he
was still unhappy; the remembrance of his dear wife
and child would always interrupt the pleasant and
smooth stream of existence. They would stand by his
bedside in his nocturnal dreams, and he would awake

pressing his dear little one to his bosom. He went back after them a distance of four hundred miles. They met one moonlight night, in the shade of a spacious oak, arranged as to the time of leaving, and the place to meet. On the selected night, when she was to bid adieu to slavery, her mistress had a party of friends; it was therefore impossible for her to get away. A disappointed husband went to the place determined upon. No wife. The next evening he went to learn the cause of the delay, but, poor fellow! he was betrayed by some innocent little negro children, to whom no blame can be attached, exclaiming, "Yonder is Uncle H——." He was sold at New Orleans, one thousand miles away again from his dear wife and child—his body loaded with chains. On his arrival there, he was put in charge of the sheriff to be taken to gaol, there to remain till a purchaser could be found. It was necessary to take off the chains, especially in a crowded city like New Orleans. Going on to prison with the sheriff, being a praying man, he asked God from the depth of his sorrowful soul to assist him to escape. He outran the sheriff, leaping over fences into fine cultivated gardens, and thus out of one into another, until the sheriff lost sight of him. The officer informed the owner of what had happened, closing his note with these memorable words:—"I will never have anything to do with another praying nigger." I trust he has kept his word. This slave came back to his old master, who owned his wife and child, intending to get them and pass into Canada. Again he was betrayed, and delivered to his late master, who bought his wife and child. They were taken to New Orleans, and all sold to one man, Deacon Whitfield, a professed Christian and a deacon of a church. Mr. H. went to a prayer-meeting without his master's consent, for which he asked and was denied; finishing his task, he went without leave, and got home before he was needed. But on his arrival his wife told him that his master had promised he should have next day four hundred lashes for disobeying his orders. What to do he knew not. He took, however, a mule, and rode ten miles into the forest, remaining there till the following night. He returned with the mule, and left it, then took his wife and child, and went in quite a different direction. The next day the bloodhounds traced them out. They were taken back. His hands and feet being tied to four stakes, his face towards the ground, the deacon had the field-hands assembled, and ordered the overseer to strike him four hundred lashes, the deacon sitting in his chair under the shade of a large tree. This poor man's wife was compelled, with the other slaves, to witness this scene, which to her was the most painful. His body was literally cut and mangled to pieces. In this condition, after being washed with salt and water, he was put in his cabin, with no doctor to attend him.

Through the mercy of God he recovered. The deacon sold him. He was absent seven years from his wife and child. His master returned to buy his wife, as he had been such a faithful servant. This man was not a Christian either. When they came to the deacon's house, after this long absence, he refused to sell his wife, and added that he would not gratify the fellow so much as to sell her to them for him. Mr. H. now spoke. That dear woman, to him the most lovely, heard and recognized his voice, though not seeing his face; she furiously rushed by her master, and fell upon him, literally bathed in tears. A woman's reign is that of love. The deacon commanded her to loose her hold. Mr. H. bowed to the ground upon his knees, and implored high Heaven in her behalf, her arms still round his neck. Her master applied the lash until he succeeded in loosing her hold, and drove the degraded slave with his master from his presence, and as long as they were within hearing they heard the screams, the moaning, imploring cries for mercy from that poor woman; never, never did he see her any more. After this he ran away from the Indian territory and came to Canada, a distance of twenty-five hundred miles. This man devoted himself to the elevation of his race in Canada for many years; he has gone to receive his blessed reward. I have heard him tell this story many times. Slavery is, as an English divine once said, " the sum of all villanies." True, this is an extreme case. But the courage, the intelligence, and the ability of the man under other circumstances, and in any other country than America, the land of his birth, would have been justly considered heroic.

But as to the separation of husband and wife, it is no exception; it is a daily, yea more, an hourly occurrence, and in many cases by professing Christians. While I write, the various professing Christian denominations of the United States own seven hundred thousand slaves, many of whom are members with themselves, and sold, in many cases, by the men that baptize them. I saw a girl sold by one of these pharisaical Christians to obtain money for missionary purposes; thus one portion of the human family is sold into perpetual slavery to evangelize the other.

"You may picture the bounds of the rock-girdled ocean,
But the grief of these mothers can never be told."

The Abolitionists are charged with exaggerating slavery, because they preach a free Gospel, and because they avow what God teaches and declares to be right, viz. equal rights to all men; because they declare that slavery is a sin not to be mitigated, but immediately and unconditionally abolished; because the churches and ministers who do not "lift up their voice like a trumpet and show Israel their transgressions, and Jacob their sins," are in dereliction of their duty, and thereby have failed to give practical demonstration of evangelical Christianity, as the true representatives of Christ. Slavery means to rob the poor of their wages, to rob men and women of their liberty (a God-given right), to rob the husband of his wife, wife of husband, father of son, mother of daughter, brother of sister, and has closed the door of knowledge against them, and deprived them of the religion of Christ. It includes licentiousness, concubinage, drunkenness, and, in short, every evil the human tongue is capable of expressing is found in the one word "SLAVERY;" it is therefore impossible to exaggerate it. Injustice may be done to humane masters by misrepresentations; but it is the men and not the system—to justify the system of slavery is to justify all I have said above; the latter is the necessary result of the former. I have been repeatedly asked, "Is not 'Uncle Tom's Cabin' overstated? Are the characters true? Are there any such characters as Uncle Tom, Topsy, &c?" As respects the former, my answer has been invariably in the negative: as to the latter, in the affirmative. As respects the facts which lie at the foundation of that world-renowned book, the subjects of Mrs. Stowe's brilliant stories, written as it were with a diamond pen, as perhaps no other can write, they are strictly correct. Seventeen years in the slave States enables me fully to understand what she says to be quite correct. The person whom she, for convenience' sake, denominates Eliza, is a living character. I lived on the Ohio River over which she crossed, and have been to the spot more than once, not, however, till after she became the subject of the story which Mrs. Stowe tells so well, perhaps in a manner that no one else can; she will be remembered by the coloured people for ages yet to come, both in the United States and Canada. After she passes from these mundane shores to a state of unsullied bliss, " where the wicked cease from troubling and the weary are at rest," she will then live in their memories. True, the names of the characters in " Uncle Tom " are assumed, their high colouring is the result of her vivid imagination; their beautiful and most wonderful construction in forming a whole, thus embellishing the story in a manner peculiar to herself, is the rich production of her refined and well-cultivated mind. But as facts, they are true. Eliza, whose real name was Mary, ran away from Kentucky; her child was truly sold, but not delivered to the purchaser; mothers alone feel the keenest pain when separated from their children; she passed many sleepless nights in her humble cottage, looking down on the face of her loved one as it innocently slept its hours away; the tears chased each other down her youthful cheeks; now and then she gave a deep and heavy sigh; to give ease to her aching heart, a flood

of tears would again burst forth; as she thought of
the parting hour, with increased vigour she pressed
her child to her heaving breast; she pressed its lips
to her own, saying, "Poor thing, mother's dear lamb
will soon be gone, what will mother do?   What will
become of her little child?   Oh, I cant live!"
Sorrow again seized her trembling frame; she sank
beneath its paralytic stroke.   Her mind was like a
dungeon dark, without any penetrating ray of light.
To her the future was much darker than the past.
She was a helpless slave, doomed to misery and woe,
for no fault of her own; and with her child she came
to the Ohio River, it being frozen over, though melt-
ing very rapidly.   The water from the melted snow
and icé on the mountains above was six inches deep
on its surface—the ice cracking both up and down
the river, trembled on the rippling waves of the fast
descending waters like a leaf on the bough of some
lofty oak dancing in the breeze.   On the bank of
that river she was at a stand-still, asking God to help
her with her child, looking behind for the approach
of her pursuers.   Beneath the breaking ice was a
watery grave; on the other side was a free land.
She entered on the icy bridge with a beating heart
and cautious steps.   With the increasing weight of
her body a large white crack, extending before her,
threatened to let her through into the water; she
leaped in an opposite direction, exclaiming, "Lord,

save me!" A similar crack would meet her there.
Again leaping from point to point, accompanying
each gigantic effort with a prayer, she reached the
current of the river, where the water runs the
fastest, the ice is thinnest, there buried in a solid
mass for roods around, seeming to let her down into
the very centre of the river. Here her efforts were
divinely invigorated, the strong arm of Omnipotence
was beneath her; she reached the shore, one hand
pressing her child to her bosom, the other clinging to
the steep bank. It was, with her, liberty or death.
Her pursuers at this moment arrived on the shore
she had left, gazing upon the object pursued, more
than astonished, profoundly confused at her success.
The massive sheet of ice broke loose from each bank,
with the thunderings of a mighty cataract; one piece
crowding upon another went simultaneously down
the rapids with accelerated velocity. Here is an
obvious exhibition of the providence of God. The
substance of this I received from her own lips. She
was sheltered by J. R., a well-known Abolitionist,
and the following night she came to my house; with
great delight and joy unspeakable I took her in.
That boy rested in my arms while going ten miles
with her to another station. This is no fiction.
Whatever you may think of the book in general,
"Uncle Tom" is true in this. The circumstances of
this young woman crossing the river at that time

were published in the leading Anti-Slavery papers of
the north, and no doubt many Anti-Slavery people
here, who read American Anti-Slavery newspapers,
have read it; the Rev. W. H. Bonner told me he
read it. This was several years before " Uncle Tom's
Cabin " was written by Mrs. Stowe. I have met
with many of these men and women whom I have
had the pleasure of aiding to the country of freedom.
In the town of Windsor, Canada, a gentleman came
and spoke to me as a friend. I knew him not. Said
he, " Don't you know me ? " " I do not, sir," I
replied. He then mentioned where I lived, and a few
incidents, which brought him to my remembrance.
Being much pleased, I said, "This is Davis." He
was dressed well, appeared quite respectable, and
could look a man in the face instead of looking on
the ground. He said, if I needed money he had a
little, and I should have part of it. Here was a
benevolent heart in the bosom of a coloured man
once a slave.

It is the opinion of some few slaveholders that
religion is a more effectual means to extort labour
from the slave than the lash. Such allow their
slaves to be taught the precepts of religion, sufficient
at least to produce obedience. Such instruction is
given orally, and no more than will effect the
subjugation of the slave to the will of his master
without the use of a severe punishment. This is

true to no ordinary extent, at least up to a certain point. Dr. Brisbane, of South Carolina, a slave-holder, testifies to the correctness of this opinion. He says, "Religion did more good to effect obedience among his slaves than a wagon-load of whips." To the honour and credit of this Christian minister, he emancipated his slaves, moved north, and became a strong advocate of unconditional emancipation. Besides, religion adds to the value of the slave. He generally sells better in the market after the auctioneer has faithfully represented the praiseworthy qualities of the slave, which consist in his physical development, his trustworthiness, his obedience and willingness to work, &c. The purchasers have ceased bidding; he belongs to the highest bidder, if none goes beyond him. The auctioneer adds, "He is a pious Christian fellow." The bidding begins afresh. Why this bidding afresh? Evidently to purchase the Holy Ghost thus represented in the slave. This is no uncommon thing. A slaveholder of this class gave his slave permission to go to church. The minister preached from the following text, "No man can serve two masters; he will either hate the one and love the other, or despise the one and cleave unto the other." The slave was unable to solve these problems. He returned home quite as ignorant as he went. Monday morning his master inquired if he went to church. He answered in the affirmative.

The master wished to know how he liked the preacher, and he answered, "Not at all." "Why?" "Because he told two falsehoods." "What were they?" "He said, 'No man could serve two masters;' I know I serve you and Master John" (his old master and his young master). "What was the other?" "He said, I would 'eder love de one and hate de oder, or I would despise de one and cleave unto the oder,' and de Lord knows I hate you boof." This, however, proves the capabilities of the slave to reason. One very cold winter's night, I was suddenly aroused by a rapid knock at my door. My neighbour had eight slaves with two horses and a wagon, which was the entire family. The Ohio river was frozen over. They brought the horses and wagon across on the ice, it being quite near to the river. It was impossible for them to travel with the horses and wagon, so I concealed the fugitives. The next day the owner was on the look-out in the town. They asked me if I knew where the slaves were. I said I did, but was under no obligation to inform him. I told him where he could get his horses and wagon. He got them by paying the expenses, the slaves not having the means of procuring them; and I had no right to them. As to the moral right of such an act of the fugitives, I have only a word to say,—that he had got a great deal more from the slaves than the horses and wagon were worth. If they had brought in their bill for every day they had worked for him without wages, and every day that they and their children ought to have been at school, I dare say he would have been quite willing to have squared accounts with them by giving them the horses and wagon. They searched in vain for their live stock, though we dared not move with the fugitives until the excitement had somewhat abated; and like many others they found their way to Canada without much trouble.

It is with grief and much pain after all our carefulness, that we lose some of our fugitives; the northern judges deliver them up to the claimants, and they reluctantly go back into bondage. In 1853, in the State of Pennsylvania, twenty-six were delivered up to the claimants, as the report of the Anti-Slavery Society of that year shows. A slave, named Jerry, was rescued from prison in Syracuse, New York, October, 1851, and at the sitting of a United States court, at Buffalo twenty or thirty persons were indicted for having participated in the rescue. Last year, a fugitive slave was arrested in Oberlin, Ohio, by being decoyed out of town, then seized by the United States marshal, and he was sent immediately on his way to slavery. The news spread like lightning, and the citizens lost no time in following these men-stealers, and at a distance of ten miles overtook them. The slave was put in the house of a Democrat for safe keeping. The people informed the proprietor as well as the slaveholder that they wanted the slave, and intended to have him, peaceably if they could, and forcibly if they must. Finding they were in earnest about it, the slaveholder came out and told them, if they would allow him to pass on without interruption, he would give up the fugitive, to which they agreed, and he was delivered up to them with triumphant shouts of joy. They, however, sent the young man to Canada. These men were prosecuted under the Fugitive Slave Bill; some were fined, others suffered imprisonment.

Justices of the peace, judges and jurors, and other public authorities, sanction the separation of husband and wife in a free State—ministers of the Gospel sanction it also by their silence. Their voices are heard against Sabbath-breaking, popular infidelity, and (especially in charging the Abolitionists with it) against drunkenness, against the Mormonite system of polygamy, but not a word against slavery, or separating husband and wife, if the people be coloured or are of negro descent. One even refused to pray for a fugitive slave who was in prison awaiting his trial; prayer on his behalf was requested at a public prayer-meeting and was refused, although at the same time requests from other sources, and on different subjects, received attention.

Escapes have been more numerous than ever

during the past year : they are augmenting continually. We add the following to show what description
of persons take their liberty :—" Twenty Dollars Reward.—Ran away from the plantation of the undersigned, the negro man *Frederick*, a preacher, 5 ft.
9 in. high, above forty years old, but not looking
over twenty-eight, stamped M. B. on the breast, and
having both small toes cut off; he is of very dark
complexion, with eyes small but bright, and looks
quite insolent, dresses well, and was arrested as a
runaway at Donaldsville some three years ago. The
above reward will be paid for his arrest by addressing
Messrs. Armont, Brothers, St. James' Parish, Shil-
lenberger and Co., 30, Torondelet Street."—*New Orleans Picayune.*

It seems from the above that this preacher was
not too pious to run away, and thus deprive his master of what he had no right to, and that this was the
second time he had committed treason against the
slave laws and Southern theology by running away.
Although a preacher, yet he would be a much better
one if free. Such advertisements as this are cut out
of Southern newspapers and put into some of the
Northern papers, so that men who are sufficiently
brutalized begin to hunt for the poor fugitives. The
Underground Railroad is doing good business, as the
following will evidently show :—" Yesterday a slave
man from Kentucky swam the Ohio river, opposite

Fulton; he reached the Ohio side nearly exhausted with cold and fatigue; as he lay resting on the shore, he observed his pursuers on horseback, with rifles, on the opposite bank.   They discovered their victim, and crossed in a ferry-boat at Pendleton, but the sight of these human tigers revived the almost drowned man, and like a deer he scaled the precipitous hill at the back of Fulton and disappeared. God speed the fugitive—and I had like to have said, crush the black hearts of his pursuers!"   This was from quite a respectable clergyman who saw the slave and his pursuers, but whose name I do. not deem it prudent to give.

The Underground Railroad pays the stockholders very well, but not so well as might be desired; but business is flourishing to their satisfaction, as the following would indicate:—"The Underground Railroad would seem to be in excellent order; a company of twenty-nine slaves from Kentucky reached here on Monday evening last, and were safely conveyed to the Canada side the next morning; they were all hale young men and women, none of them over thirty-five years of age, for whose capture we hear liberal offers proclaimed.   They travelled by wagons through Indiana (a free State), and reached here in good condition."

The *Detroit Christian Herald* says, "The Underground Railroad is pre-eminently qualified and well

adapted to do business for a long time, we hope as
long as a slave remains in his chains to weep." "Lord,
Thou hast heard the desire of the humble, Thou wilt
prepare their heart; Thou wilt cause thine ear to
hear, to judge the fatherless and the oppressed, that
the men of the earth may no more oppress." God
prepares ways and means for the escape of the slave
to Canada. A slave passing from New York State
into Canada was put on board a ferry-boat at Black-
rock, near Buffalo, by an Abolitionist; at this junc-
ture the master came up and saw his slave on board,
bound for Canada; the boat was just receding from
the shore; he drew his revolver, saying to the ferryman, "If you don't stop, I will shoot you." The
Abolitionist who put the slave on board, and paid
his way over to Canada, drew his revolver, and, pointing it to the ferryman, said, "If you do not proceed I
will shoot you." * The ferryman, finding himself
between two fires, said, "I will die doing right." He
went on, and in a few minutes the slave was beyond
the grasp of the tyrant. David very appropriately
declares, "God will judge the poor and needy, He
shall save the children of the needy, and shall break
in pieces the oppressor." I would rather be in the
condition of the slave than the slaveholder when God
shall avenge himself on the evil-doer – and the slaveholder is one. · "He shall deliver the needy when he

* Neither of them fired a shot.

crieth, the poor also, and him that has no helper. He shall redeem their souls from deceit and violence, and precious shall their blood be in his sight." The slave is poor and needy—God delivers him from the iron heel of inhuman oppression. His retributive justice will not always be shown in silence, but will eventually waken the guilty slaveholder as from an ominous dream, and break upon his head like the thunderings of a cataract or the roarings of the Niagara. Sometimes slaves that are invalids take it into their heads to escape. A woman who had a husband with only one leg, managed with the assistance of some good friends to have him removed to Canada; her master flogged her every day during an entire week for the purpose of extorting from her a confession as to her husband's whereabouts; too true was she to the higher dictates of human nature to betray the trust reposed in her by him whom she loved so dearly; she endured all like a faithful Christian, ever true both to her husband and to her God. Finally she was among the missing, but found herself in Canada with her husband; though she had him to maintain, she was free, and in a country that recognized her freedom. If slaves run away who have only one leg, we may expect escapes to be more numerous with those who have two legs.

I am indebted to Mrs. LUCIE S. DAY for the following :—

The mansion of Mr. Hayes was pleasantly situated on one of the bluffs which form a part of the bank of the Mississippi. On a certain evening, at that mansion, all the pride of that section was gathered. Sounds of revelry and mirth echoed through the apartment; bright forms flitted by the open windows; and woman's low, musical laugh told of happy hearts within.

Away from this crowded scene, near the bank of the river, stood Clara, the daughter of Mr. Hayes. But why is she not with the other daughter of his, the admired of all? Her features, you see, are as perfect, her eyes as intelligent, her form as graceful, as that other sister's. We soon learn—she is a slave. That settles all the mystery.

Another form approaches her—a tall youth; and as he approaches, he whispers to her, "My sister!" She looked up with a smile, but soon an expression of anxiety passed over her face, for she saw a stain of blood upon his breast, and on his brow the traces of recent passion. His eye even then flashed with fire.

"Charles, what is the matter?"

"Matter! Are we not slaves—mere ciphers—who dare not call our lives, our souls our own? Nothing belongs to us but thought and feeling. I will yet escape, and tell my wrongs to those who will hear and sympathize. Hush! Do not tell me God is just. I never felt his justice. What I am, they have made me; and if I sink down to deep despair, I sink under the pressure of their tyranny. All that I have learned, all that raises me above the brute, I gained myself, being my own teacher. I knew they wished me not to read, yet to do what they wished not, was pleasure. Do not think me wild. I have been tempted almost beyond what I could bear. A little while ago, as I sat on yonder rock, gazing upon the bright stars, I wondered if they were worlds, inhabited like ours; and if so, were slaves there? There came many bitter thoughts. I spoke aloud; when suddenly I received a blow in the face, followed by these words: 'Slave, let that teach you what to think!' I rose from the ground almost blind with rage; and there stood Master Henry, grinning with pleasure. It was too much. I glanced at him, then at the steep bank; something within me whispered, and I obeyed. With all the strength of madness and revenge, I seized and held him over the water. Another instant, and he would have floated a mangled corpse on the dark waves of this river. But I looked down, and saw the reflection of the stars on the water,—they looked like your bright eyes. I thought of you, and spared him. But come to our little cottage; we will collect a few things, and long ere the morning light we will be far hence."

Clara threw her arms around her brother's neck

and, bending her head low that he might not see the tears, said, "I cannot go. Do not say I do not love you. Whom else have I to love? Our mother is dead; our father is worse than none. I have no one to love but you. I dare not render your escape doubtful by going with you." . . . . .

The morn was near its dawning, and still Clara knelt in prayer. Her uplifted face was covered with tears; her accents fell not unheard on the ear of Him who hath said by the mouth of his Apostle, "And if we know that He heareth us, whatsoever we ask we know that we have the petition that we desired of Him." Clara seized hold upon that promise, and she felt that her entreaty for her brother's safety would be answered. She arose from that long communion with God, and with comparative cheerfulness went about her daily task. When it was reported that Charles was to be found nowhere on the plantation, and even when the company of hunters went forth with bloodhounds, pistols, and the other accompaniments which slavery uses on such occasions, Clara's faith remained unshaken.

But let us look forward and watch the fate of that brother. All night he has been making his way through the thick forest; now parting, with already lacerated hands, the vines that clustered in his path, now crawling through the dense underwood;—he made his way, until the bright sun peeped through the overhanging leaves. Plunging further still into the forest he came to a brook which he crossed and recrossed, and then threw himself down to rest in the welcome shelter of a canebrake. Here he lay still and unmolested until near noon, when he heard the bay of the leader of the hounds, which had separated from the others, and reached the stream. In he dashed; again he crossed, and came on through the rustling cane. Charles's heart beat wildly—he shuddered; but it was only for a moment. Drawing his knife, he waited in silence the coming of his savage foe. The animal approached, and, for a moment, shrank beneath the acknowledged supremacy which flashes in the eye of man. Charles seized that moment, and, catching the dog by the neck, buried the knife in his throat. He gave a low bay, and all was over.

Charles had saved himself for a short time, but at a great risk; for when his pursuers discovered the dog, they would be certain that the fugitive was near. Just then, as he heard the baying of the dead hound's companions, there was a rustling near him in another direction, and a great animal of the wolf kind appeared, falling upon the dead dog to devour him. Charles, recrossing the brook as noiselessly as possible, pressed on until he was compelled to rest from pure exhaustion.

He remained until he was aware by the quiet

around that his pursuers were gone. Thanking God in his heart for his preservation, he pursued his toilsome way until he found a place of rest on the free shores of Canada—British monarchy being freer than American republicanism. . . . . .

Yes, indifferent as a majority of the American people are to the claims of humanity, honour, and justice, and apostate as are a large portion of the politicians, ministers, and church members, to the principles of Republicanism and Christianity, with reference to their treatment of slaves and the coloured people, it is to us a cause of profound gratitude to that Great Being who declares that " He is no respecter of persons." He has raised up a company of men and women to contend for truth and freedom against the combined influence of false democracy and impure Christianity; and to wrestle against principalities, against powers, against the rulers of the darkness of this world, against spiritual wickedness in high places. Thanks to God for all the success he has given to efforts begun and continued in his name, in accordance with his Spirit, and in reliance upon his promises. It is obvious to every intelligent and candid looker-on, that the anti-slavery cause, in spite of the sneers of opponents, the denunciations of men in power, and the designs of the crafty, is steadily pursuing its march to a glorious consummation. Its progress may be retarded by

diabolical cupidity, cruelty, and knavery of demons
in human shape, who kidnap, enslave, or torture their
unoffending and helpless fellow-men, in foreign lands,
on the high seas, during the coffle-march between the
States of the American Union, or on the cane-fields
and cotton plantations; by unprincipled politicians,
who rise to power on pledges to befriend and enlarge
the area of despotism; or by the hireling press, pros-
tituted pulpits, corrupted courts, and the multiform
classes whose God is Mammon. It has been so retarded. But the seeming triumphs of these enemies
of the human race is transient: "He that sitteth in
the heavens shall laugh; the Lord shall have them
in derision." Truth is mighty, and will prevail. The
rights of man will be regarded, oppression shall cease,
both body and mind will be unshackled, "the expecta-
tion of the poor shall not perish." "The mouth of the
Lord hath spoken it." The slaveholders may drive
the free coloured people from their comfortable homes
in the slave States as exiles, as some are doing, in
order to tighten the chains still firmer on the necks
of the suffering vassals; but let these men remember
we can plant ourselves at the very portals of slavery.
We can hover about the Gulf of Mexico, nearly all
the isles of the Caribbean Sea bid them welcome;
while the broad and fertile valleys of British Guiana,
under the sway of the emancipating Queen, invite
them to their treasure and to nationality. With the

Gulf of Mexico on the south and Canada on the north, the latter is already a receptacle for fugitive slaves, waiting their more intelligent free coloured brethren to join them in breaking the galling yoke from the bleeding necks of their yet suffering bondsmen, and they may still keep within hearing of the wails of our enslaved people in the United States. From these stand-points we can watch the destiny of those we have left behind. Americans should also remember that there are already on that vast continent, and in the adjacent islands, a large population of coloured people, who are only waiting the life-giving and organizing power of intelligence to mould them into one body and into a powerful nation.

The following tabular statement exhibits an approximate estimate of the numbers of coloured persons of the African race to be found on the North American Continent. The free populations are distributed in the different countries in the following proportions :—

United States	3,650,000
Brazil	2,250,000
Spanish Colonies	1,470,000
South American Republics	1,180,000
British West Indies	750,000
Hayti	50,000
French Colonies	270,000
Dutch ditto	50,000
Danish ditto	45,000
Mexico	70,000
Canada	60,000

It thus appears that nearly three-fourths of the whole African population in the western hemisphere are still ground down as beasts of burden under the galling yoke of slavery. May the efforts of the fugitive slaves contribute their full measure of moral influence against this accursed system; and, under God, may they be made instrumental, in some degree, in hastening the time when all men shall be recognized as being entitled to that freedom which is their birthright and their just inheritance!

PASS HIM ON!

A LAY OF THE UNDERGROUND RAILROAD.

Pass him on!   Pass him on!
Another soul from slavery won;
Another *man* erect to stand
Fearless of the scourge and brand;
Another face now lifted up,
Lips that drink not sorrow's cup,
Eyes no longer dimm'd by tears,
Breast no longer fill'd with fears;
Limbs that have no galling chain
Their free motions to restrain;
Back no longer bow'd and scored,
But with birthright now restored.

He that late the burden bore,
　　Felt the lash and pangs untold,
To be chattelized no more,
　　Barter'd, given, bought, or sold—
　　　　　　　　　Pass him on !

Pass him on !　Pass him on !
Every man who hath a son,
Every woman who hath borne
Child, and hath a heart to mourn
O'er the woes by others felt ;
Every maiden who hath knelt
Down in prayer for brother dear,
Or a loved one yet more near ;
Every youth who hath a friend
With his thoughts and hopes to blend,
And desireth aye to be
Both in speech and action free ;
　Every one who hates the wrong
　　And would vindicate the right,
　Help the weak against the strong,
　　Aid this brother in his flight—
　　　　　　　　　Pass him on !

Pass him on !　Pass him on !
Ye whose sires the sword have drawn,
And with blood your freedom bought ;
Ye by whom the truth is taught,
That the God who dwells on high,
Sees one human family
In the races of mankind,
And would all together bind
In one unity of love,
Blissful as the life above ;

Ye who speak and wield the pen,
Eloquent for rights of men,
   And would proudly spurn the thought
     That if you had skins less fair,
   You might then be sold and bought,
     And the galling fetters wear—
              Pass him on!

Pass him on!   Pass him on!
Though his foes be legion;
Though the bloodhounds on his track,
Yelling, strive to bring him back;
Though man-hunters from the south
Threat you with the pistol's mouth,
And the federative law
Would your spirits overawe.
Heed them not—imprisonment!
Take it, and be well content;
Heed them not; endure the fine;
Grow, through sacrifice divine;
   Do as you'd be done unto,
     Careless of the consequence;
   Keep the higher law in view;
     Heed not ruffian violence.
              Pass him on!

Pass him on!   Pass him on!
Let him lie your couch upon;
Give him raiment, give him food,
Give him kindly words and good;
Watch and guard his hours of rest;
Hide him from the searcher's quest.
Through the city wrapp'd in sleep,
O'er the river broad and deep

By the farmstead, through the vale
Lighted by the moonbeams pale;
O'er the prairie wild and wide,
Where the red men still abide
  (Hunters these, but not of slaves—
    Far more merciful than they);
  Storms and tempests, winds and waves,
  Nought the fugitive must stay.
                Pass him on!

Pass him on! Pass him on!
Crime hath he committed none.
Would you have him grovelling lie
In the bonds of slavery?
Nobler far to rend in twain
And throw off the yoke and chain:
Nobler through darkness grim,
Dangers thick besetting him,
Freedom thus to seek in flight,
'Scaping from the gloom of night
Unto freedom's glorious morn;
From the darkness to the dawn
  Leapeth he o'er chasms wide.
    Help him all who help him can,
  God the north star for his guide
  Giveth; every fellow-man—
              Pass him on!

            H. G. ADAMS.

Rochester, England, 1854.

CONDITION OF THE

FUGITIVE SLAVES IN CANADA.

As misrepresentations in some instances have pre-vailed respecting the true condition of the coloured population of Canada, I have been induced to make the following statements, which are derived from per-sonal knowledge. If these promiscuous suggestions will in any way gratify the friends of the slave, and serve the cause of freedom, strengthen the hearts and hands of British Christians in the glorious work of emancipation, my highest expectations will be fully realized, and my soul will rejoice in the Lord.

Perhaps you, who have been cradled in a land of liberty, cannot altogether enter into the feelings of those who breathe the air of freedom for the first time. The slaves, upon their arrival in Canada, gaze with delight upon a land of freedom. Would you believe it, tears often flow from their eyes; they lift their voices and weep aloud. It is a glorious thing to gaze for the first time upon a land where a poor slave, flying from a so-called land of liberty, would in a moment find his fetters broken, his shackles loosed; and whatever he was in the land of Washington, beneath the shadow of Bunker's Hill, or even Plymouth Rock, here he becomes a man and a brother. But even here, it is too true, they find they have only changed the yoke of oppression for the galling fetters of a vitiated public opinion. True, they come to Canada exceedingly ignorant; but who can wonder at it, born as they are to an inheritance of misery, nurtured in degradation, and cradled in oppression; with the scorn of the white man upon their souls, his fetters upon their limbs, his scourge upon their flesh? What can be expected from their offspring but a mournful reaction of that cursed system which spreads its baneful influence over both body and soul, which dwarfs the intellect, stunts its development, and debases the soul?

If you look upon your map, you will clearly see how Canada is divided from the United States, in some parts only by a narrow boundary. Some of the States just over the boundary are free States; yet, if a fugitive slave be found there, he is taken back to his former owner, and his bondage made still harder.

But let them once be within the Canadian boundary, they are free,—they are safe,—for they are then under the protection of our gracious Queen. The population of Upper Canada is nearly 1,000,000. The most densely populated portion is from the ex-

treme south-west, in a straight line along the Great
Western Railway as low down as Toronto, on Lake
Ontario, a distance of 250 miles. This embraces a
large scope of country, from the south-west of Lake
Erie, along Lake Huron west, as far north as Lake
Simcoe. This is considered, not without good reason,
the best farming region of Upper Canada. Of this
population 60,000 are coloured people, who are almost
entirely in Upper Canada, because of its close connection with the States, 15,000 of whom are supposed
to be freeborn, and at various times to have removed
from the free States of America into Canada, to enjoy
equal rights and privileges with the white citizens,
which they could not do in any portion of the United
States. Making due allowances for the Canadian
coloured people, we still have a population of 45,000
fugitive slaves from the United States, and this
number is augmented yearly at the rate of 1200.
These are, as it were, only a drop taken from the
ocean of 4,000,000, now in that Republic which boasts
so much of its freedom,—liberty for the white man
and slavery for the black man,—" Liberty for the
slaveocrats, and a strong hemp rope for the eloquent
throat of an English Spurgeon," should he be found
in that land of blood, preaching the Gospel to every
creature. The coloured people are mostly located in
towns, villages, and townships, in the region above
described.

There seems to prevail among them a disposition
to settle in villages and towns, especially those who
have been porters in stores, warehouses, or waiters in
private families, their object evidently being to obtain
situations in their former occupations; failing, as
many do (which is not to be regretted), they, in
the latter case, do what they should have done in
the former, engage in agriculture. However, experience soon teaches them that they are in the wrong
place; consequently a larger proportion now settle in
agricultural districts than formerly. I may say, the
majority are thus engaged, perhaps not in every case
from choice but the force of circumstances; in either
case, however, our object is accomplished. I am decidedly of opinion, that in Canada, as in all countries,
being settled with emigrants, agriculture is the occupation; therefore, we perpetually urge upon them the
importance of thus becoming their own proprietors.
There seems to exist a peculiar fondness for each
other, which is characteristic of the coloured race;
this influences them to settle together, thus forming
large colonies, or settlements as they are called. Land
is purchased from Government, by individuals and
companies, at one dollar and a quarter per acre.
They divide it into sections, half sections, quarter
sections, and even eighths of sections, as convenience
may require. These speculators sell this land at two
dollars and two dollars and a half per acre, giving the

purchasers the advantage of ten years to complete the payment.

Any man with a little industry and economy can secure himself a home, as many do, or Government will grant fifty acres as a homestead, on certain portions, and in certain places, to any one who will settle thereupon, giving a simple fee deed to the settlers, when their cabins are erected on the spot selected. But this land is, in the interior districts, a great distance from market, without even roads along which to convey their produce to market. To settle in such districts requires some capital to commence with, which the poor have not, and those who are so fortunate find it to their decided advantage to settle as near a good market as possible.

The consequence is, the coloured people, with the whites of equal condition, buy land of the speculators, and remain within reach of markets, their prosperity depending, in a very great measure, upon their own industry. It may be said, to the credit of many of our coloured brethren, that they have bought land by paying a few pounds in advance, and many of their farms are in a good state of cultivation, and, in some instances, superior to many of their white neighbours.

In the county of Kent, many are engaged in agriculture, residing upon and cultivating their own farms. One farm near Chatham, of which place we shall speak hereafter, formerly owned and cultivated by a coloured man, recently deceased, is regarded, even by those not so favourably disposed to the negro race, to be the model farm of the community. It is now cultivated by his family, and still retains its former character.

It is a generally-admitted fact in Canada, that the coloured people are much better farmers than the Irish, or even Canadian French. The better portion live in two-story frame houses, painted white on the outside; now and then there is a respectable barn on the premises, around which are fowls, hogs, horses, cows, and occasionally sheep, but less attention is paid to the latter than to any other kind of stock. The majority live in log-houses of one room, in which a looking-glass, one or two bedsteads, a bureau, &c. may be seen. A garden is usually connected with the house, in which vegetables grow luxuriantly; here the mistress occupies herself from two o'clock in the afternoon till five in the evening, and perhaps later. I am decidedly of opinion, that no people could do better under similar circumstances than the fugitive slaves and the coloured population are now doing in Canada. I often think many of the friends of the negro race expect too much in too short a time from the emancipated. The growth of a nation is slow, especially when degraded as the African race is. The nefarious system of slavery has entailed upon them almost inconceivable

evils, which requires generations to eradicate, while
they are only in the first generation.

> "Oh ! speed the moment on
> When wrong shall cease ; and liberty,
> And love, and faith, and right
> Throughout the earth be known,
> As in their home above."
>
> WHITTIER.

As the foregoing remarks are of a general character,
we will now enter more minutely into particulars,
which, in all probability, will be more satisfactory to
the reader. Toronto, as we have said before, is situated on Lake Ontario. It is a flourishing town, admirably adapted for a commercial city. The census
returns of 1850 gave a population of 50,000 ; it is now
supposed to be about 80,000, of which 1600 are coloured, or of the African race. Of the latter number
1000 are fugitive slaves. The coloured population are
engaged in various avocations ; there are blacksmiths,
bricklayers, carpenters, six grocers, one physician, also
shoemakers, painters, &c., one broom manufactory,
and a large coal and wood yard, kept by a coloured
gentleman.

A considerable number, who emigrated to Canada at
an early period, are in comfortable circumstances. Mr.
A., who came from Mobile, Alabama, eighteen or
twenty years ago, has, by his industry and economy,
accumulated 100,000 dollars in property. He has now
retired from business, and his three sons are studying

for the medical profession. I am exceedingly happy
to add, that few men are more respected than he, not
because of his wealth only, but for his piety also. Mr.
M. owns two lines of omnibuses, and horses and carriages. Dr. T., mentioned above, has quite a respectable drug-store, in one of the principal streets, which
no gentleman of his profession would feel disgraced
to enter. An ice-merchant, who furnishes hotels,
public-houses, and private families, during summer
with ice, has a farm under good cultivation. His son-
in-law has, on the same farm, a two-story frame house,
furnished as well inside as it is finished outside.

The winters are long and intensely cold in Canada,
during which but little out-door work can be done,
which causes a deal of suffering among the poor. To
remedy this to some extent, soup-houses are established, from which they can obtain coal, wood, bread,
and soup. In the winter of 1858, only one coloured
family made application for assistance. However, we
must take this fact into consideration, that the necessities of this class are, to some extent, supplied by a
few benevolent friends, who interest themselves in
their behalf, but not sufficiently to prevent numbers
of them from applying for assistance from the town
fund. Many, too, would rather, and absolutely do,
suffer much, before they will make known their condition, or apply for aid to their white friends. Even
considering all these things, it is to be supposed, in a

population of 1600, many and frequent would be the applications. But the true cause is found in the fact that there is a great disposition in the better classes to assist their less fortunate brethren, and that they are very industrious.

Hamilton, at the head of Lake Ontario, around which the railway trains pass to the Niagara Falls, New York, and the eastern States, has a population of 24,000, 600 of whom are coloured people. Among them are blacksmiths, carpenters, plasterers, and one wheelwright. Many of them own property, but how much or to what extent I cannot say. Mr. M., a mulatto, who still drives his own hack, is worth 15,000 dollars. He came to Hamilton seventeen years ago, and acted as porter in a store twelve years; he then bought a hack, and he has now two carriages and four horses. He takes three newspapers, one weekly and two daily. On the 14th of January, 1859, he said to me, "I shall have to emigrate to the West Indies to educate my children, for, the other day, my two daughters were refused admission into the female academy, because they are coloured." This may startle some, but it is nevertheless a lamentable fact; prejudice so prevails against the coloured race, even in Canada.. In communities mainly consisting of Englishmen and Scotchmen it does not prevail to the same extent, therefore, the more emigration we have of these classes, the better for the coloured people. I am persuaded if these were a majority in Canada, no prejudice would exist. May God hasten the period when the glorious text shall be fully realized, " He is no respecter of persons, but every one, in every nation, that feareth God and worketh righteousness, is accepted of Him." As to their general morality the following will suffice:—In 1858 there were 1982 arrests and summonses to appear before the court; of these 81 were coloured. Putting down the population in round numbers at 24,000, the proportion of arrests would be about one in 12½, estimating the coloured population, for convenience of calculation, at 550, would be a fraction over one in seven. The fact of their being almost exclusively emigrants, the proportion of adults among the coloured people is greater than the population at large; some deduction must, therefore, be made from their proportionate criminality. Beggary and pauperism are almost unknown among them. Not a coloured person in this place is supported by the township. They feel their position and know that they are on their trial, and that they have a character to establish and maintain.

St. Catherine's, perhaps about thirty-two miles from Hamilton, is a straggling town of about 2500 inhabitants; 200 or 250 will include the entire coloured population. I am not so favourably impressed with the prosperity of the coloured people here. Their morals, I am sorry to say, are much lower than in most towns and settlements; there is more drunkenness than we usually see. There are among them a few good Christians,—pious, devoted persons; but a kind of goodness without intelligence. One man owns two hacks and four horses. It seems the community has been left without competent teachers to instruct the people; the consequence is, they have not done as well as we could desire. I may add, that several of them own property, and are in comfortable circumstances; but, upon the whole, they are far behind the mass of their brethren.

London is a town still further west, on the Great Western Railway; it has a population of 12,000, of which 500 are coloured people. What I have said of them in Toronto and Hamilton will apply to their brethren here. They are rapidly advancing in this place in general refinement and respectability; nearly all seem engaged in some sort of useful employment. This is the missionary field of the Colonial Church and School Society. They have done and are still doing a great deal to promote the interest and elevation of this people. I am confident God has blessed the various agencies and means employed by them in this glorious work, and I hope He will continue to do so. I only regret that they are not sufficiently catholic. In London the coloured children go to school with the whites; the latter feel themselves not disgraced by the association. For the want of such Christian-like union, many of the coloured children are growing up in ignorance, even in a land of freedom, and so it will be until they are able to establish and sustain their own institutions, as I hope, by the grace of God, ere-long they will. The elevation of a people depends more upon themselves than upon their neighbours. I have long been convinced the sentiment of the eminent poet is quite true :—

> "They that would be free,
> Themselves must strike the blow."
>
> COWPER.

These people are perfectly willing, and manifest a disposition, to receive instruction, as the following extract will demonstrate. I quote from the report of the Church School Society for 1859, page 27 :—

"The tracts are still valued by the poor fugitives who can read. They are sometimes returned to be exchanged, with such expressions as the following :— 'That's a nice book, it is so sweet and comforting.' 'I thought the last my daughter read to me was the best I ever heard in my life,' said a poor fugitive the other day. A mother said, 'That tract you lent me was so good and so beautiful that I lent it to a friend of mine, and that friend lent it to another friend, and so it has gone through twenty people's hands, and it has not come home yet.'" I shall give my testimony in a subsequent page.

In conversation with the heads of the police in the

town of London they said that petty crimes were more frequent among the people of colour than any other class, except the Irish, who were much worse. However, this was a mere opinion, as, in the statistical statements of the police department, the offences committed by the coloured people were not separately recorded, as in some other towns. They further said, beggary and pauperism were unknown among them. I thought this quite a free and open concession, and spoke well for them, which I found to be quite true when visiting their families. Mr. J. is a fugitive slave, from North Carolina (my native state). He settled in the town of London twenty-three years ago; he became a merchant, but is now a dealer in medicine. He has a good drug-store, and is possessed of considerable property.

Chatham is a town situated at the head of navigation on the river Thames. Unlike Toronto, Hamilton, or even London, it has but few fine buildings, and its appearance at first sight would not very favourably impress a stranger as to its wealth; nevertheless, there is more business done here than would seem upon first entering the town. There are three saw-mills, two shingle-mills, two potash factories, three cabinet warehouses, four flour-mills, several iron-foundries, three breweries, &c. It is a port of entry, and exports a large amount of lumber. This busy town contains a population of 6000,—2000 are coloured people, who seem to add their quota to its industry. One gunsmith, four cabinet-makers, working on their own account and employing others, six master-carpenters, and a number of plasterers; three printers, two watchmakers, two ship-carpenters, two millers, four blacksmiths, one upholsterer, one saddler, six master-shoemakers, and, last of all the trades, a cigar-maker.

Chatham is the head-quarters of the negro-race in Canadá. It has acquired considerable notoriety, even in the United States, because of the great number that have settled there. The better class live in such houses as before described—two-story frames, painted white outside; numbers of their unfortunate brethren live in log-houses, with gardens around them, well stocked with vegetables. They have here two day-schools, though not very well provided for; one has eighty pupils, the other thirty. They seem to be under good training and instruction. They probably have the largest, if not the best conducted Sunday-school in Canada among the coloured people. I had the pleasure of addressing three hundred children in this school, which is considered a large number to be in attendance. It is certainly conducted in such a manner as to perpetuate a lively interest among the scholars, which is an essential element to the prosperity of any school. The other school is well conducted, but not so large. The reciting of passages by the pupils from both the Old and New Testament Scriptures, was a sufficient evidence of their aptitude for learning, which the negro race has ever evinced when surrounded by favourable circumstances.

There are two chapels in Chatham, Methodist and Baptist; the former has quite an intelligent coloured minister. The latter has no regular pastor; I have occasionally preached for them. The *Press* is conducted by a coloured gentleman, well adapted to the business, the continuance of which up to the present time is owing to his industry and economy; though it is not at present in a very encouraging condition, that is no fault of his. Newspapers usually depend on voluntary subscription for support; it is, therefore, a very difficult matter to keep one in existence among an uneducated people, as this class is in Canada, when its support, entirely or in part, is to be derived from them. Parents do not see the necessity of taking papers for the benefit of their children who can and are learning to read; in the majority of cases, if they did, they would not have the means to pay for one. However, I may truly say, in some respects, and with the best of feeling for my brethren, "they have eyes to see and see not, and ears to hear and hear not." We need more schools and qualified teachers in Canada; and as the people advance in intelligence, we may have more newspapers and editors. The schools are very irregularly attended, just as they

attend to everything else, in the most erratic manner
imaginable. However, knowing as we do the cause
of it, we bear with greater fortitude their imperfec-
tions. Our hope for better things is from the rising
generation now entering on the great theatre of
human existence, whose minds are still to be developed, and their characters to be moulded; and
unless we are prepared with efficient facilities to
meet these emergencies, they will still be, intellec-
tually, infants. We believe that the period will
arrive, ere long, when they will be enlightened, vir-
tuous, moral, and intelligent, or, in other words,
possess those qualities in a higher degree than they
now do, and lavish their blessings among the various
kingdoms of the earth as freely as they have lavished
on them their chains and ignominy. Education, combined with Christian civilization, will enlighten, refine,
and elevate the down-trodden sons and daughters of
Ham.

The hearty loyalty of the coloured population in
Canada is attested by all that come in contact with
them. They love the country that protects them in
the free and untrammeled exercise of their natural and
inalienable rights. The following anthem is the production of a man who was a slave twenty-three years,
now living in Chatham, Canada West:—

AIR,—HOME AGAIN.

Bless the Queen ! England's Queen ;
  Heaven protect and save !
Oh, may the space be wide between
  Her cradle and the grave !
Ever may her land remain
  Asylum of the free,
A spell to break each galling chain
  Of human slavery !
    CHORUS,—Bless the Queen, &c.

Beneath her sway, equal rights
  Extend to rich and poor ;
From halls of dukes and gallant knights,
  To the humble peasant's door.
Hence ever from the peasant's cot,
  And domes of wealth and sheen,
One prayer ascends of word and thought,
  God save, God save the Queen !

O'er her may angels spread
  Their all-protecting wing !
Oh, may they shield her heart and head
  From each delusive thing !—
Shield her from the gloom and care
  By mortal eye unseen,
That she may live—long live—to wear
  The crown,—God save the Queen !

When her long and peaceful reign
  Shall here have been complete,
And she for brighter realms would fain
  Leave this terrestrial seat,
May her deathless spirit soar
  To that bless'd world-of light,
Where ills and cares disturb no more,
  And there's no day nor night !

        J. M. BELL, Chatham, C.W.

{ Fifty-four miles further west, on the Detroit river, which connects Lake Erie and Lake St. Clair, is situated the town of Windsor, which has a population of 2500. Few towns, perhaps, in Canada are older than this; it is the place where the larger portion of the fugitive slaves first arrive on British soil, because of its close connection with the States. This portion of Canada is divided by the river Detroit from the State of Michigan; across the river, at this point, unknown numbers of slaves have passed into a land of rest, where the slaveholders cease to trouble them, and the baying of the negro hounds is no more heard on the track of the flying fugitive. From 700 to 800 is the number of coloured people in this town; among them, as in other towns, are carpenters, shoemakers, bricklayers, grocers, &c. Most of them are doing well, and quite a number have comfortable homes for their families; but they are not extensive property-holders, as in some of the places mentioned before. Mr. O. has a large provision-store, and does extensive business, much more than any other coloured gentleman in the town; he is therefore very much respected by them. He lives in a neat, well-furnished brick-house.—Rev. W. Troy, my colleague and fellow-labourer among this class, owns property in this town, also a farm in the country. Here is mainly his field of labour, where he is now erecting a chapel with a school for their benefit. The Lord has abundantly

K

blessed his humble efforts in bringing many to a knowledge of the truth as it is in Christ Jesus. He is the leading man among them.—Mr. B. has been employed at the railway-station for four or five years. He has not been absent a single day, unless prevented by sickness. By his steady habits and faithfulness to labour, he has won for himself a high respectability. —Mr. Lewis Clark, who was her Majesty's mail-carrier from Windsor, across the river to Detroit, in the State of Michigan, is a fugitive slave, from the State of Kentucky, but, to the disappointment of his employers in the post-office, he was necessitated to give up that useful and respectable occupation. His former master having been informed of his locality and avocation, notwithstanding several years had elapsed since he left Kentucky, pursued him to the very borders of Canada, watching his return with the mail in the city of Detroit, on the States side, anxious to lay violent hands on the poor man, to bind him in chains, and take him into slavery again. Fortunately some friends informed him that his late master was waiting on the other side for his return. Oh, what a blessing to him and his poor wife, that he received this timely information! Of course every precaution was taken to ascertain the facts of the case, but every advancing step only served to confirm the truth of the statement, until it was found absolutely dangerous for him to continue in his employment. The slaveholder dare not cross over the boundary line to claim a fellow-man as his property in Canada.

> "Slaves cannot breathe in England:
> If their lungs receive our air,
> That moment they are free."

Mr. Clark, by his industry and economy, has accumulated considerable property. He has also money in the Bank of Upper Canada. He is distinguished for his piety and benevolence: but few men in his position contribute more for the spread of the Gospel among his people, which at once achieves for him the universal respect of his brethren. Mr. Clark was fortunate enough to escape with his wife,—children they have none. She is a woman of very superior mind, quite different from the generality of slaves. Her condition was one of the exceptions. She was a domestic servant, quite a favourite in the family, consequently permitted many privileges, among them the privilege of learning to read. She was intrusted with everything in the house, newspapers and books not excepted; to the reading of these she devoted much of her time, which now proves a greater blessing to her than it possibly could have done in a condition of slavery; by means of this knowledge she gained her freedom. Her master, in conversation with the Rev. W. Troy, mentioned above, said, "He often told his wife that permitting Anna to read 'Uncle Tom's Cabin' (which he as a humane man had purchased for his own family circle), she would be induced

K 2

after a while to run away." Now, said he, " if she had
never read ' Uncle Tom's Cabin,' I should have had her
and Lewis to-day, as my slaves." Thank God for
" Uncle Tom's Cabin"! These are not the only persons
it has been instrumental in redeeming from the galling
yoke of slavery. Her Christian qualities, no doubt,
won for her good usage, and many kind words from
the family to which she belonged. Many persons
would therefore think she had little cause for escaping,
which I admit ; but the fact of her being a slave is a
sufficient justification. I have often heard her say she
was treated as well as a slave no doubt could be treated.
She was especially attached to the family, but when
the thought would occur to her mind, " What right had
she and her husband to be slaves to another, for no
crime whatever, save the colour of their skin, in which
they had no choice ? " this was sufficient to make her
unhappy all her life long. "My Bible tells me, ' God
is no respecter of persons ;' why, then, should I be a
slave to another ?   I can read as well as my mistress,
I can reason as logically, I can think as clearly ; why
should I not think, reason, and act for myself?   A
knowledge of my condition makes me unhappy, independent of my good usage from humane owners. It
is slavery I hate, and not my owners." On hearing
these noble sentiments fall from the lips of a person
once a slave, and in a manner most insinuating, with all
the dignity of the most refined and cultivated person,

and with an indignation expressive of the deepest
abhorrence for the nefarious system of unmitigated,
inhuman chattelism, I surely felt I was in the presence of a superior being.

Persons without trades, in this town, as in others,
find sufficient employment at white-washing houses,
fences, cutting and splitting wood, working in gardens,
digging wells, &c., for all which labour they get from
four or five shillings per day. They also get a fair
portion of the public works. When the Grand Trunk
Railway was being constructed, about 1500 hands
were employed, 500 of whom were coloured men. I
consider this quite a fair proportion. About ten miles
from Windsor there is a settlement of 5000, which
extends over a large portion of Essex County; of this
settlement some places are more densely inhabited than
others. It is called the fugitive's home. Several years
ago, a very enterprising and intelligent fugitive slave
came to Canada, bought a large quantity of land from
the Government, divided it into small lots, from one to
twenty acres, and sold it to his brethren as they arrived
from the States, giving them from five to ten years to
complete their payments. This induced many to settle here, by purchasing in this small way. Any one
could buy less than an acre, but not more than twenty
acres. Emigrants settled here in such numbers, principally fugitives, that it is called the fugitive's home.
Perhaps the larger portion of this land is still un-

cultivated, while a great deal is in a high state of
cultivation, and many of the people are doing well.
This plan answered the purpose very well, at that
time, and no doubt it was the best that could be
adopted under the circumstances; but since the land
monopolists in Canada have become more numerous,
and there is consequently more opposition in this kind
of speculation, the same class can purchase from these
monopolists from the eighth of a section to any indefinite numbers of acres, with the same period to make
payments. Thus they become much larger proprietors, and have sufficient quantity of land to augment
trade by raising live stock, such as hogs, cows, horses,
sheep; or by cultivating grain, beans, peas, Indian
corn, wheat, and hay, all of which are saleable, and,
when turned into cash, enable them to pay for their
land. Many in the fugitive home with mere garden
spots, have either rented it to their neighbours or left
it to go to wreck, and have bought, leased, or rented
much larger farms elsewhere, which I think upon the
whole is infinitely better than the former, while the
course pursued by the fugitive in the previous case is
not to be lost sight of. It shows a spirit of enterprise
and a disposition to trade, a philanthropic feeling for
the elevation of his degraded brethren, which he fully
carried out in his own conduct during his life. He
was the leader of his race in that portion of Canada.
In the fugitive home are two schools built of hewed

logs; perhaps there is school three months in the year
but oftener none at all, sometimes for the want o
teachers, at other times for want of money to pay
teachers.

Government pays only one half of the teachers
salary, the other portion the parents in the districts
are responsible for. The teachers must collect themselves. The fact is, they seldom have school. The
school-houses are used for worship on Sundays, when
they can get preachers, but few preachers like to go
into the backwoods: if they did they would not like to
go through snow, very often half leg-deep, or knee-
deep. Therefore they have but few sermons during
winter. Upon the whole there is a great amount of
spiritual bareness, and intellectual ignorance. As for
industry, I find no fault, in general. Intelligence
does not by any means keep pace with the industrial
habits of the coloured people of Canada. That is to
say, they are more inclined to industrial habits than
they are to intelligence.

Sunderwich, a few miles from Windsor, has two
thousand inhabitants, four hundred, perhaps, coloured, who are mostly engaged in agriculture, though
living in town; some own farms, others work by the
day in lumber-yards sawing wood, others devote
their time to gardening, which pays very well, and
some few are grocers. They have a chapel, but no
school-house, more for the want of teachers than

otherwise. In the counties of Kent and Essex, which contain more coloured people than any other counties in Canada, they are prevented, by a legal enactment of the provincial parliament, from educating their children with the whites. They must, therefore, build their own school-houses, select their own teachers, pay half the salary of those teachers, and the Government the other half. The elevation of the negroes under such disabilities can be but slow even in Canada.

Amherstburgh, sometimes called Malden, is situated on the banks of the Detroit river, twenty miles from the city of Detroit, about which I have previously spoken. This town has a population of about 2000, probably 800 of whom are coloured people. This place, with others in this part of Canada, is not so prosperous as some other portions. A great many of the French are settled here; in Lower Canada the French are very intelligent and refined, but here they are very uncultivated,—they are quite a different class altogether. The coloured people are principally engaged in agriculture throughout this region of country, the western portion of Upper Canada. Colchester, New Canaan, Sandwich, and many other places where the coloured people have settled, seem to be developing the resources of the country.

I might merely allude to the Dresden settlement, thirteen miles from Chatham; this place is quite prosperous, having well-cultivated farms, &c. Chatham is their nearest and best market. In this settlement, my brother missionary has just finished a small chapel, which has been in progress for four years, but no school-house; I suppose he will keep school in the chapel. The houses here are mainly log-houses, but they are generally, well furnished, and exhibit considerable taste.

Wilberforce settlement is fifteen miles from London.—One word as to its origin. Previous to 1829, a great many coloured people moved from the slave States into the State of Ohio, which, up to 1845, had laws preventing coloured people from living therein, but many came into that State, being ignorant of the existence of such an enactment. In 1829 this law was put in force, and 1000 coloured people were driven out of the State. Previous to their emigration, they sent a deputation to the Governor of Upper Canada, to ascertain whether or not he would allow them to settle in Canada. I copy his reply:—

"Tell the republicans on your side of the line, that we royalists do not know men by their colour. Should you come to us, you will be entitled to all the privileges of the rest of his Majesty's subjects.
                    "SIR JAMES COLEBROOK."

This people, knowing that Wilberforce was a friend to their race, named their colony after him.

This colony, as a farming region, is surpassed perhaps by few; they live in good houses generally, and pay more attention to stock than in most of the settlements. The people have more information, and are proving their capabilities for self-government.

A remark or two relative to the Elgin settlement: —This is decidedly the most improved of any colony in Canada; it numbers perhaps 800 coloured people, with a chapel and school. The school has been in regular operation for several years, the Rev. Mr. King being their instructor. God has abundantly blessed his labours in bringing many to a knowledge of the truth as it is in Christ Jesus, and also in developing their intellects, and moulding their characters, by which they have unquestionably demonstrated their original capacities for self-government. I much regret that we have not more such faithful servants of God among the coloured population of Canada; we suffer more than can be imagined from the want of such qualified teachers. He is pushing forward their elevation still further; may God bless his efforts in the future as He has done hitherto! Only one arrest for crime in that community, among the coloured people, has occurred from 1850 to the present time.

It would be my pleasure to enter more extensively into their condition, but in a mere sketch like this it is impossible; besides, travelling from place to place, as I do, I cannot give the time and attention the subject requires. I have already protracted my statements to a greater extent than I first intended; however, my only object has been to present facts derived from personal observation, without any attempt whatever at a display of learning or talent, of which I cannot boast. I must now redeem my promise given on a previous page. The negro mind is peculiarly susceptible of religious impressions, and much may be hoped and looked for from the planting of Christianity in a soil so favourable to its development. Naturally, the negro is gentle, teachable, humble, and simple, physically and mentally enduring, which he has beyond a doubt proved, by patiently enduring the galling yoke of inhuman oppression on the North American continent for two centuries. They receive a dying Saviour's love with alacrity and joy,—the faith which hopeth all things, believeth all things, loveth all things, they embrace readily, because it best accords with their warm and overflowing sympathies, and unsuspecting, kindly natures. They are easily moved to tears on religious subjects, such as the crucifixion of the Saviour, the joys of the world to come, &c.; these are themes upon which they are most easily brought into sympathy. In the midst of a sermon they seem literally enchanted, their eyes set upon the speaker, some with their mouths open, with all the simplicity of children, occasionally exclaiming, "Thank God!"

" Amen!" "Thanky Jesus!" Others shout aloud,
"Glory to God in the highest!" fall on the floor,
and some, more self-possessed, shake each other's
hands, saying, "I am free both soul and body." The
minister pauses until the flash of excitement abates,
and when they resume their seats he proceeds as
before, commencing where he left off. To suppress
the manifestation of their feelings, would be a means
of destroying their happiness.

It is a great privilege to stand forth and proclaim
the Gospel of salvation to hundreds around you rescued from slavery, both soul and body, and invite
them to enter into the glorious liberty of the sons of
God, where they will see their blessed Saviour, and
receive a happy congratulation, "Enter into the joy of
thy Lord, prepared for thee from the foundation of
the world." "These are they that have come up
through great tribulations, and have washed their
robes and made them white in the blood of the Lamb."

I wish, if possible, to disabuse the minds of many
who are not favourably disposed towards the negro
race, or who have only a superficial knowledge of
their condition; they seem to think the negroes are
a nuisance, or, in other words, they are so numerous,
that the Canadians are at a loss to know what to do
with them. It is true some persons in Canada seek
this method of venting their spleen upon this helpless
and unfortunate race; but it is not true that they have

become so numerous as to baffle the skill and judgment of the inhabitants as to their well-being. I
would much rather have them flood the cold and
dreary region of Canada, free, than have them continue in the sunny climes of the slave States, in
the miserable condition of unmitigated slavery,
gradually sinking beneath the bloody lash of unfeeling tyrants into their graves, only to be remembered
by their friends with sorrow, many of whom are destined to share the same mournful fate. Yankees who
live in Canada, Americanized Canadians, also many
of the Irish, when coming in contact with coloured
mechanics and labourers generally, who are as well
skilled in their profession and business as the former,
and perhaps much better, complain very much indeed. Sometimes liquor-dealers, who are patronized
more by these classes than the negroes, join in the
unpopular complaints. If the coloured people sell
their produce cheaper in market than some others,
they also complain, "Too many niggers here—they
keep the price down in the market—if they continue
to come, I don't know what we shall do," &c. These
vile calumniators should remember what the negroes
lose in the price of their produce, they may make up in
the quantity they sell, and thus demonstrate a talent
for trading. These are the character of the complaints, and the source from whence they emanate.
It is quite obvious that it is a mere jealousy of

business competition. I think I am quite justifiable
and within the range of human probabilities in saying, not a newspaper editor in Canada would feel free
to subject himself to public censure by uttering such
aspersions upon the coloured population.   On the
first of January, 1859, in conversation with his
Excellency the Governor, Sir Edmund Head, on the
progress of the coloured people, he made the following very significant remark, "We have plenty of
territory for these emigrants."   On the 12th of the
same month, in conversation with the Governor-
General, at his residence, he asked me "if it was my
opinion that the fugitive slaves were on the increase
in their emigration in Canada?"   I answered in the
affirmative.   He said in reply, "We can still afford
them homes in our dominions."

The provincial parliament recently incorporated an
association as a body politic, for the education of
coloured youths in Canada, of which I was appointed
a member of committee, to write the constitution.
I have only room for the preamble, which simply
shows the object of the association:—"Whereas a
charitable association has for some time past existed
in this province, under the name of 'The Association
for the Education and Elevation of the Coloured
People of Canada,' having for its object the education of the coloured youth of this province, and their
training and preparation for the active duties of life;

and whereas it is expedient to encourage to the utmost so laudable an undertaking, and the said association having represented that by being incorporated they would be enabled greatly to extend their philanthropic labours, and more easily manage the affairs and business thereof, it is expedient to incorporate the said association, to grant the usual powers of bodies incorporated for like purposes, therefore her Majesty," &c. If these facts, derived from the highest authority in the country, are in any respect an exponent of public opinion in Canada, they evidently show the public in general are in favour of such emigration, which is in direct opposition to the false representations often made,—that they don't wish any more such people, &c. Canada needs and must eventually have a sufficient number of labourers, such as the coloured people, to develope her resources, and bring the land into cultivation, by which its value will be enhanced, both to the interest of the owner and the Government. Taxes assessed for governmental purposes are in proportion to the value of the property thus taxed, consequently the higher the state of cultivation into which this land is brought, the more profitable it is to the Government. Therefore every possible encouragement is held out by Government for emigration—fugitive slaves, as well as others. It is to be hoped these evidences are quite sufficient to satisfy those who have been misled on this point. If you prevent the slave, flying from his chains and handcuffs, entering Canada, where he is free, under the Magna Charta of the British constitution, which knows no man by the colour of his skin, I ask for the slave, and in the name of humanity, where will you allow him to go ? What shall we do with the 1200 coming northward every year, seeking freedom if haply they may find it ? Will you be so cruel, so fiend-like, as to send them back into perpetual bondage ? "God forbid!" They will run away more and more, in spite of all the fugitive-slave laws that the American Government may pass.

I have elsewhere confined my remarks to the better class of the coloured population, in order to show their capabilities of self-government and civilized progress.

We will now speak more especially of the mass and their condition. On their arrival in Canada they are in a perfect state of destitution, among strangers, and in a strange country. You who are accustomed to travel, even with means to supply your various necessities, know what *you* feel on arriving for the first time in a foreign country where every face on which your eye falls is strange. There arises in the mind a kind of lonely feeling, and a desire to be at home; but, alas! it is far, far away. You are by these reflections prepared, at least in some degree, to sympathize with those who have fled from taskmas ters, cruel drivers, the bloody lash, the clanking of handcuffs, and, above all, the unrighteous laws that sanction these evil practices. They have sought and happily found a home sacred to freedom. In many instances they find themselves surrounded by many sympathizing friends—friends, they are well worthy of the name—many of whom have drunk deep of oppression's cup, but, through the providence of a kind Heavenly Father, have reached their much-desired haven, like their brethren kinsmen according to the flesh, whom they now shelter. They are made welcome to their new homes, and receive many happy congratulations. It is to them soothing balm poured into their wounded souls and much-depressed spirits. Our first duty is to supply them with food and raiment, such too as are best suited to the climate into which they have just come. In almost every case they are destitute of both. The coloured population are expected by the white citizens to perform these duties, or at least bear the burden of it, from their identity with the sufferers. We have more emigrants in autumn and winter than any other season of the year, from the obvious reason that the facilities for effecting their escape are pre-eminently better then than at other periods. We are quite happy to receive them at any time, winter or summer, day or night. Though we are very much burdened with increasing responsibilities, yet our

souls leap for joy when one succeeds in reaching this
virgin soil, Canada. As the mass of the people are
themselves poor, they are unable to meet the entire
demands continually made upon them. The more
benevolent of the community who are interested in
the moral and religious elevation of this class, assist
them, which contributes much to the alleviation of
their suffering, and makes the responsibility much
easier with us. After we have put them in positions
suitable for employment, we feel ourselves very
much relieved. There is a kind of independency
which is rather commendable,—they like to have
the name of administering to their own necessities,
and it is to them a self-mortification when unable
to do so. This may not be applicable to some—
I think it is not—but it prevails to a very great
extent.

Even with the aid of many good friends in Canada,
we are still unable to meet the demands as they
increasingly crowd upon us. The Abolitionists of
the northern States, say from Boston and New
York, have sent over boxes of clothes, old and new,
and of all sizes, which have been a great blessing.
Very many have been relieved who would have
suffered almost beyond human conception but for
the timely aid thus afforded. These contributions
are voluntary, and are by no means regular, nor indeed do we expect it, though much desired. But

the Anti-slavery friends are burdened from year to year in sustaining their papers and periodicals, lectures, &c.; the consequence is, we have a very great amount of distress, and distress unavoidable, and, as may be expected, considerable mortality among these immigrants.

I was called upon, one day in mid-winter, by a man for a testimonial setting forth his suffering condition, that he might make applications to the benevolent of the community for assistance, without which, from a minister or some well-known and accredited person or persons, such applications would be to little or no purpose; but before doing this, I made myself acquainted with the truth of what I was called upon to certify. For this purpose I immediately visited his family—his representations were quite true; even worse than he had said. I found in a miserable hut, which I will not attempt to describe, his wife and five children, whom they had been fortunate enough to bring with them from slavery. Two of the children were crying, as she said, for something to eat; the poor woman weeping bitterly because she was unable to supply their wants. She said, "Sir, I have repeatedly prayed God to send us friends: I hope you are such a one." I said, "If I can do anything for you, I shall be most happy to do so." After a few questions as to her condition, her faith in Christ, &c., I asked her if she had ever been reduced to the like

L 2

condition before. Her answer was substantially as follows:—"When I was in slavery my two eldest children were sold a short distance from me; I was not even allowed to go to see them, nor were they allowed to come to see me. I thought I should die with grief; I prayed God to take me out of the world; then I thought it was wrong to do so. I remembered hearing my mistress say Canada was a place where all the coloured people were free; then I prayed God to enable me to get there. Not knowing what moment my husband might be sold from me, or me from him, we made up our minds to run away; during the Christmas holidays we asked our master for a pass (his written consent) to go and see our children, which he kindly granted. We took our children and immediately started for Canada: we were twelve weeks coming; we prayed and travelled. Many a time we would eat corn by the way." She said, "I have not that for my children now." She paused for a moment, and burst into tears. We were all silent for the time being; her husband could no longer restrain his feelings at the truthful recital of this sad story, which is only one among thousands. Her feelings in some degree subsiding, and gaining her self-possession, "This," said she, "was worse than my present condition." Said I, "Very true, you are free: but had you not rather be in slavery and have enough to eat, without begging as you have to do?"

"No, no, I had rather be free and crawl on my hands and knees from door to door." I could not but admire her high-mindedness and love of freedom. I need not tell you we immediately supplied her with provisions Here were two Christian persons who had not attended a place of worship for sixteen months, not for want of holy zeal, of strong and growing desires to do so, but because their condition would not allow them.

We have a great many, both religious and irreligious, suffering in this respect, more from the want of suitable clothes to fit them for the weather, and to attend public worship, than the want of food. The latter cases are so numerous, we are unable to supply them. To meet them the best way we can, we hold meetings in their dwellings on week-evenings; they will assemble in each other's houses when they are absolutely unprepared to do so in public. I knew a man whose constitution was totally undermined by consumption, from exposure to the cold, half-naked, endeavouring to maintain his family. Poor man! he finally died; but, thank God, he died in the full triumphs of Christian faith. I was in the habit of visiting the family of a pious good man, as I supposed, in whom I was not mistaken; but not seeing him attend church (as we call all places of divine service church), I began to think I might possibly be mistaken in my good opinion of him. I inquired as to the cause; he said, "I have not clothes suitable to go to church;" pointing to those he had on, he said, "these are all I have." I evidently felt, from what I saw, the cogency of what he said. A great many devoted Christians, with whom I have been acquainted, were thus prevented from attending the house of God for the same reason. Even our Sunday-schools, as well as day-schools, where we have them, a great number of the children cannot attend because they are not thus prepared. In cases of Christian people, I have known the better class to lend clothes to their poorer neighbours to attend worship, and the clothes thus lent returned.—Feb. 28, 1859.

The Report of the Fugitive Mission in Canada has the following article,—I use it in confirmation of what I have said:—"There is more than an ordinary amount of distress prevailing in Canada at the present time, and failure of the crops last year has caused considerable rise in the price of provisions in this city (London); the poor, both white and coloured, are suffering severely." The Report goes on to say what we all too well know is the inevitable effect of slavery. From the general improvident habits of the coloured people many of them are in a wretched condition, both as regards food and clothing. The few boxes just received will enable us to minister to the wants of many in the latter respect, and to some extent alleviate their sufferings. I am sure the benevolent Christian friends who have placed it in our power to do so would feel themselves more than repaid could they witness the looks of gratitude and listen to the expressions of thankfulness given by the recipients of their bounty. Parents lose many of their children by exposure. A woman in Toronto said she had lost six, another four, all from consumption; this is the disease of which they mostly die; when once seated in the constitution, its victim lasts a short time, therefore it has received the appellation of quick consumption. As to the destitute children of Amherstburgh, Mrs. Hurst says:—" Children go about the streets with apparently nothing on but an old cotton frock; no wonder they get sick and die. A woman told me yesterday she had lost ten children by consumption." It is not to be understood that Canada is an unhealthy country by any means, for the contrary is the fact. This mortality of which we are speaking is from absolute destitution, which could be avoided if we were able to meet the cases with sufficient food and suitable clothing; neither are we to infer that the coloured people can't live in Canada because of the intensity of the cold. True, it is severe, especially on those coming direct from the south, as the majority do; coming into a climate much colder than they have been accustomed to, even when clothed suitable to the climate, they suffer very much for two or three winters at least, after which they become acclimated, and are as healthy as any people.   But, on the other hand, when not properly clothed they must suffer prodigiously, and many, as we have said, certainly die.

To the readiness of the coloured people to receive the Gospel, which they on all proper occasions evidently manifest, we have already alluded; we add the testimony of the Rev. Dr. Willes, Professor of Divinity at Toronto College :—" There are about 60,000 emancipated slaves settled in Canada, most of whom have fled from bondage.   I have repeatedly preached to congregations of emancipated slaves, and ever found them attentive and devout.   They appear to me to enter with more spirit into the praise of God than white men generally."   Dr. Willes is an earnest and a true friend to the coloured people in Canada ; he has very frequently preached for my congregation, and does now during my visit to this country ; he, as also Mrs. Willes, have relieved the sufferings of many on their arrival in Canada; they very often visit the houses and supply their necessities.   They are bold and fearless, willing to teach and instruct them in the knowledge of God, attend their meetings both religious and political, ready to give all necessary and good advice.   These are the kind of friends we need in that country, and among such a people.

Having said so much relative to the coloured people of Canada, we will say a word as to Canada itself. The province of Canada extends over an area of

242,500 square miles, or 240,000,000 acres, and is consequently one-third larger than France, and nearly three times larger than Great Britain and Ireland. The settled portion is about 40,000 square miles; the entire population in the Canadas exceeds 2,500,000. That part of Canada east of the Ottawa River is called Lower Canada, the inhabitants are chiefly of French extraction; this part of the colony comprises 160,000,000 acres, of which not more than 15,000,000 have been surveyed. Of Upper Canada, west of the Ottawa River, the majority of the population are British; an enormous system of lakes form a network of water communication over the entire province, and a line of rivers connect the inland lakes with the sea, so that the most distant recesses of Canada are within reach of trade and navigation, and large vessels can proceed a distance of 2000 miles inland. The lines of railway are the Great Western and Grand Trunk, with a few other still shorter lines, altogether about 849 miles. The reader has now before him a geographical bird's-eye view of this great province, possessed by nature of many very great advantages quietly waiting the indefatigable hand of human industry to develope them for the benefit of the inhabitants. The two great wants of Canada are capital and production. We are happy to say, the capitalists of England and Scotland are emigrating there much more than formerly; and all the more

necessary, because of the influx of the fugitive slaves
and free coloured people from the States, with whom
they come in direct contact and aid in their elevation,
and it is still more necessary because the former know
nothing of American prejudice against colour, which
is contrary to all law, both human and divine.   The
resources of this country must be developed, it therefore requires labourers to do that; there is sufficient
room for such labourers from all countries.   The
fugitive slaves and the free labourers can all find
ample space on which to settle and labour; the
former are coming in almost 2000 yearly.   They
have been brought up in the manual-labour school,
out of which they have come to Canada; they need
not be taught how to labour, but may be taught
economy to direct and regulate that labour to the
best advantage.   This is a forced emigration; nevertheless, I am happy to say many are honourable and
worthy colonists.   We look anxiously forward to no
distant day when Canada will be the brightest gem
in the crown of our world-renowned Queen.   We
have the territory, the lines of rivers and chains of
lakes for navigation; we are gradually getting the
capitalists, and the labourers still faster.   In the advancement of any country, three agencies are essen-
tially necessary—the Bible, the Church, and the Press.

Civilization, without Christianity, makes but slow
progress in any portion of the world.   Human go-

vernments are only correct when based upon the great principles of the Bible and influenced by the doctrines of the Cross. They then become the living and resuscitating elements of the whole machinery. Therefore the prosperity of a nation depends upon its conformity to the Word of the living and true God. In this respect, England may be proud—perhaps this is too strong a term; but in this she may rejoice and praise God. I verily believe her national prosperity is the result of her tenacity to the Word of God. An African king sent an ambassador to England to inquire of her Majesty what was the secret of England's greatness, he standing in her august presence. She presented to him the Bible, saying, "Tell your king this is the secret of England's greatness." This act speaks volumes in favour of religion. This Bible is quite sufficient to raise benighted Africa to the same eminent and praiseworthy position, by its undying influence; she once walked hand in hand with her sister nations in the advancement of Christian civilization. This noble act again speaks volumes in the acknowledgment of equal moral, religious, and political rights of that degraded race, which the United States most decidedly refuses to acknowledge. Our gracious Queen was not ashamed nor afraid to stand in the presence of one of the sable sons of Africa, and from her own hand presented to him the precious Word of God. The Church is the mighty agent,

under God, to accomplish this great work. To her
God gave this Word and said, "Preach the Gospel to
every creature "—to the savage, the rude barbarian,
the cultivated Greek, the North American Indian, the
American slave, the proud and haughty Anglo-Saxon
—yes, "to every creature," without respect of persons; this is the duty of the Church. "Preach deliverance to the captive." The press is the great
circulating medium through which she speaks to
thousands in one breath, and sends truth over a whole
empire with lightning speed; thousands of volumes of
God's Word are cast abroad among the nations of
earth's teeming millions, by means of which we can
converse with distant friends. Through the press the
justice of God is vindicated—truth, love, and mercy
shown in their true positions and relations—the social,
civil, and political rights of man are advocated. The
press is a means of drawing out the latent energies of
the human mind, and of placing man in his legitimate
and proper position before the world.

People with sufficient courage to leave the house of
bondage, and to succeed in reaching a land of freedom, as the fugitive slaves have done, should have
these mighty agents to promote their happiness in
their new homes, which they prize so dearly. They
have the Bible, but it needs to be more generally circulated among them. Religious knowledge should be
circulated more freely. We have the Church, but her

cords need strengthening, and her borders extending. We have the press, but not in direct contact with the coloured people, and devoted to their special interests, except the one to which I have already referred.

I therefore hope, by the blessing of our common Lord, that the coloured people in Canada will eventually be established on a more solid basis, and thereby be fully prepared for the higher duties of life, by means of which they may exert a reflexive influence upon the nefarious system in the United States, and thus aid in the great work of human emancipation.

APPENDIX.

SLAVERY originated in a spirit of gain, by which it is alone sustained. It is thought the same agency is the only effectual method to overthrow it in the United States. If not the only effectual one, to my mind it is certainly one that should not be overlooked by Abolitionists struggling against this gigantic evil; they should eagerly and earnestly lay hold of everything, and adopt every method consistent with Christianity, that would effect its final abolition. The profit derived from the culture of cotton is the chief support of slavery in the United States, for whatever shall prove available in making slave labour unprofitable must of course cause the demand for that labour to cease. To accomplish this result by means of the cultivation of cotton by free labour, should be the object of the friends of the slave, not with motives to injure the slaveholders, but to free the slave. I doubt not but much more cotton would be cultivated by the slaves in a state of freedom than is now cultivated; it is quite obvious that a man will do a greater quantity of labour, and better in quality, by the stimulus of wages, than by the force of the lash. If a white man is prompted to labour by the love of gain, it is very clear to my mind a black man will do the same; the love of gain is an innate principle of human nature, and is not therefore confined to any class or complexion of individuals; only assure them they will receive a just remuneration for their services, and there will be no lack of labourers.

Dr. Cooper, of South Carolina, in his letter on political economy, estimates the labour of a slave at two-thirds of what a white labourer, at usual wages, would perform. Put a slave in a condition of freedom with the white labourer, he would perform as much labour; consequently the demand for cotton, both in the home and foreign markets, would be amply supplied with cotton by free labour, whereas it is now supplied with slave-grown cotton.

The following will give the reader an approximate idea of the value of the slaves in cash, and what the claimants annually realize from their labour. I cut the following from the *New Orleans Delta*, a slave-holding paper, published July 11, 1857 :—

"The slaves, numbering over three and a half millions; their value, at present prices, sixteen hundred millions of dollars. The cotton plantations the south is estimated at eighty thousand; the aggregate value of their annual products, at the present prices for cotton, is fully one hundred and twenty millions of dollars. There are over fifteen thousand tobacco plantations, and their annual products may be valued at fourteen millions of dollars. There are two thousand and six hundred sugar plantations, the products of which average more than twelve millions of dollars. There are five hundred and fifty rice

plantations, which yield an annual revenue of four
millions of dollars."

The above evidence shows that cotton by far exceeds
all the other staple products of the sunny south, both
in number of farms and annual income. The number
of slaves engaged in the cultivation of each article is
something like the following:

Rice	125,000
Sugar	150,000
Tobacco	350,000
Cotton	1,815,000
Total	2,440,000

These slaves are engaged in the cultivation of articles to supply foreign demands, and out of them all,
cotton is the strong pillar upon which slavery commercially rests, in the United States. Think of it—
over 1,000,000 slaves engaged in the cultivation of one
single article, COTTON, averaging more than 220 to a
plantation, drivers applying the lash at their will upon
the tender persons of females as well as males.
Think again, that five-sevenths of all the cotton con-
sumed in England is cultivated by these slaves. The
threads of which your garments consist are stained
with the blood of the slave; the driver buries the
bloody lash in the quivering flesh of his victims,
extorting their unrequited labour to add to your comfort; in order more effectually to do this, the slaves
are kept in ignorance. Give them knowledge, they
will free themselves. Think of it! You buy chains,
handcuffs, and whips, by which the slaves are punished.
Yea, you do more than this: you pay for the slaves
themselves, by purchasing cotton. Four million bales

of slave-grown cotton are sold in the British market annually; this amount increases as the demand increases. The price of slaves varies with the price of cotton. "When cotton is 14 cents per pound a slave is worth 1400 dollars; every cent per pound adds a hundred dollars to the value of the slave." Such was the statement of Mr. Walker, in which he was quite correct. Hence an immense forced emigration takes place between the slave States. It is calculated that 30,000 slaves, or more, are bought and sold annually; tens of thousands of poor slaves are torn from their husbands, wives, and children, precipitated upon the cotton-growing States, swelling in many localities an already overcrowded population. On many a plantation and in many a slave-coffle there is heard " a voice of lamentation and weeping, and great mourning; Rachel weeping for her children, and would not be comforted, because they are not."

I have no doubt but the foreign slave trade is quietly in operation in the United States, in confirmation of which I quote the *New Orleans Delta,* which declares most positively it is so:—"African slaves are imported into Mississippi and other seashores. In Mississippi there is a market for African slaves, and on plantations in that great and enterprising State, negroes annually imported from Africa are at their daily work."

These Africans are bought by the planters, and you pay for them by paying for the cotton they cultivate. The amount of mortality on those plantations is alarming, known only to those who are conversant with them, the necessary results of being overworked and under-fed; when so they are without

M

legal redress; consequently the average life of the slave on the cotton farms is fourteen years, and on the sugar plantations seven years. Here is the sacrifice not only of comfort and happiness, which the slaves have as good a right to enjoy as ourselves, but of life itself, simply to augment our happiness, and to promote the interest of the *owners*. I have repeatedly seen slaves ordered to the fields to work before it was sufficiently light to weed cotton without cutting it up and then flogged because they did cut it up, and work at night as long as they could see how to work without injury to the plant, which is very tender, and must be treated accordingly. As to the regulation of labour, the laws make the following provision:—In South Carolina, "Whereas, many owners of slaves, and others who have the care, management, and overseeing of slaves, do confine them so closely to hard labour that they have not sufficient time for natural rest, be it therefore enacted, that if any owner of slaves, or other persons who shall have the care, management, or overseeing of slaves, shall work or put any such slave or slaves to labour more than fifteen hours in twenty-four hours from the 25th day of March to the 25th day of September, or more than fourteen hours in twenty-four hours from the 25th day of September to the 25th day of March, any such person shall forfeit any sum not exceeding twenty pounds, or under five pounds, current money, for every time he, she, or they shall offend therein, at the discretion of the justice before whom the complaint shall be made."—2 *Brevard's Digest*, 243.

Georgia.—"Any owner of a slave or slaves who shall cruelly treat such a slave or slaves by unnecessary or excessive whipping, by withholding proper food or nourishment, by requiring greater labour from such slave or slaves than he, she, or they may be able to perform, by not affording proper clothing, whereby the health of such slave or slaves may be injured or impaired, every such owner or owners of slaves upon sufficient information being laid before the grand jury, whereupon it shall be the duty of the attorney or solicitor-general to prosecute said owner or owners, shall, on conviction, be sentenced to pay a fine, or be imprisoned at the discretion of the court."—*Prence's Digest*, 376.

These provisions are of no practical value to the slaves whatever. The whole matter is a well-arranged systematic scheme of diabolical hypocrisy. No slave, and no free person of colour, can be a witness against a white person in any case. The planters are not expected to prosecute each other for ill-treatment to the slaves. The overseers, who do the flogging and order the working, are not apt to inform against each other, dependent, as they are, on the planters for employment. Many of the non-slaveholding whites at the south are a servile and degraded class, like the overseers, depending upon the slaveholder for labour to support their families; therefore they dare not inform against the abuser and have him brought to justice. In the name of God and outraged humanity, how is the slave to have redress under such circumstances? It follows, they may be worked any number of hours in the day at the will of the drivers, Sundays not excepted, and in all kinds of weather. I have repeatedly seen them working on the Sabbath, especially in planting tobacco, as this must be done

in rainy seasons, and in the spring of the year; should
it rain on Saturday night the slaves are ordered out
in the field on Sunday morning to set the plant. The
first gang of slaves I ever remember seeing at work
on Sunday, was on a tobacco plantation; my young
and untutored mind revolted at the sight; but by
frequent repetitions of the scene I soon became inured
to it. Familiarity with sin tends to harden the human heart and blunt the moral sensibilities.

The same hypocritical provision is made relative to
the food of the slaves :—Louisiana: "Every owner
shall be held to give his slave the quantity of provision
hereinafter specified, to wit,—one barrel of Indian
corn, or the equivalent thereof in rice, beans, or other
grain, and a pint of salt ; and to deliver the same to
the slaves in kind every month, and never in money,
under a penalty of ten dollars for every offence."—
Martin's Digest, p. 610.

You see there is no meat, sugar, coffee, or tea,
mentioned in this act. This barrel of corn is in the
ear as it comes from the field ; when shelled, it
amounts to one bushel and a half, or forty-eight
quarts, which is to last a slave one month, with one
pint of salt; allowing thirty days for a month, it would
be equal to one quart and three-fifths per day. This
is to be reduced to meal, which would be a little
more than a pint per day. With this they must work
fifteen hours per day one part of the year, and fourteen hours another. The prisoners in the state
prisons, whether for life or a shorter period of time, are
fed on substantial food, and quite sufficient in quantity, three times a day ; and seldom, if ever, are required to labour more than ten or twelve hours per

day. Though this act mentions no meat, I have known the planters to allow the hands from a pound to a pound and a half of meat per week. Many, not having utensils in which to cook, broil it on coals of fire; put it with a morsel of bread into gourds; take it to the field, which is to last them all day. Mothers, two weeks after childbirth, must be in the field making a full hand, in many instances putting her child in the shade of a tree, permitted to nurse it twice a day, though it may cry from the sting of insects. She may plead for permission to nurse it; the overseer may grant it, or he may not; if so, it is considered very kind of him indeed. Reader, bring this matter home to your own heart, then think and feel for the slave. Thus he suffers to cultivate cotton for your benefit as well as others. I could write volumes on the plantation life of slaves, which I have said nothing about in my book, because it was foreign from my subject. Ye mothers of England, can you do anything at this distance to alleviate the condition of your sisters on those cotton plantations in that country? Can you pour the oil of joy into their hearts? Cease as soon as practicable the use of cotton bathed in their tears, chasing each other down their sorrow-worn cheeks; then you will have snatched the bloody lash from the hand of the wicked driver and dashed it into a thousand pieces. The gory wounds now bleeding while I write will be joyfully healed with the oil of gladness from your hands. You will have sealed up the fountain of tears which for centuries has been opened; you will have placed your sisters in a position where their chastity can be protected as yours now is; you will have struck the

death-blow to this giant evil. I appeal to you because
you can do much in this matter. I appeal to you because the slave cannot. I plead the cause of the
widow and the orphan. "I open my mouth for the
dumb." The power of turning the scale against the
tyrants and in favour of freedom, commercially speaking, is in the reach of England's mighty grasp. England is depending on America for cotton. Millions
of her people are employed by means of it. The
existence of thousands hangs upon this feeble thread.
It is with the slaves whether they shall live or die;
it is with the slaves in the United States whether
they shall walk the streets of this beautiful country
perfect vagabonds, or be employed in making an
honest living. Suppose the slaves were to cease cultivating cotton unless they were paid for it, which
they have a perfect right to do, what would become of
millions now depending on them for a living, who are
employed in manufacturing the raw material which
they cultivate? What would the capitalists do in
Lancashire? Their large manufactories must be
closed; your streets would be filled with beggars, the
dying and the dead. The very moment the slave declares, in the strength of his God, he will cultivate
cotton no longer without wages, England's commercial
operations must cease; starvation would pervade the
land; as mistress of the seas, her mighty ships
would be compelled to haul down their sails. The
whole country would be literally clothed in sackcloth
and ashes. You may say it is not likely the slaves
will do so. I think it very probable God may raise
up another John Brown more successful than the
former. The slaves have attempted, in another State,

since John Brown's death, to break their chains.
There are half a million of free coloured persons in
the United States, daily growing in wealth and intelligence, one in interest and feeling with their suffering
brethren in the south, a large portion of whom emigrated from the slave States, and are willing at a
moment's warning, when necessary, to place themselves at the head of four millions of slaves, and, with
the incidental aid of sixty thousand in Canada, in
defiance of their distardly claimants, would lead them
to the very borders of Canada. With this view of
the subject, say not it is impossible or improbable.
I speak of it not as a scene to be desired, but one
within the range of human probabilities. " The chains
of the slave will be broken, let the hammer come
from heaven or hell." Let England extricate herself
from this awful dilemma. If the cotton crops fail
in the United States by any means whatever, let it
be their own failure, and not England's ; but now
such a failure would affect England as well as
America! Let Britain become self-supporting respecting cotton, by cultivating free-labour cotton ;
besides, she would free the slaves thus engaged in
the cultivation of this article. To emancipate one
million would be a death-blow to the entire system.

It is no longer a question whether free labour is
cheaper than slave labour, or whether England has
soil to produce it or not ; but what is the best plan
to accomplish the desired object. I am glad to learn,
from the last report of the Cotton Supply Association
of Manchester, that the subject is eliciting the attention of members of both Houses of Parliament, and

has obtained the assistance of the chief department
of Her Majesty's Government; the British consuls
in foreign ports are giving the scheme their attention
and kind consideration. It is quite pleasing in one
respect to see the cotton crops have only doubled in·
twenty years. For the benefit of those who may read
this book, and may not read the report, I extract from
it the following:—"We must point to the fact,
that although in 1840 the çrop of the United States
was 2,177,835 bales, and in 1860 it may reach
4,500,000 bales, the growth has only been doubled
in twenty years; while the number of spindles employed in this country and on the continent was, in
1840, 27,266,000, but in 1860, 69,642,000." In other
words, while the increase of growth has been doubled,
owing to the high prices of almost exclusive markets,
the increase of spindles has more than doubled by the
enormous addition of 15,110,000, requiring an additional one million bales to give them employment.
The position of the trade is therefore, in 1860, so far
as America is concerned, worse by one million bales,
than it was in the year 1840. It is not necessary to
allude to the numerous places that produce cotton
both in Her Majesty's dominions and beyond them;
nor yet is it necessary to refer to what has been ex-
pended and what experiments have been tried in
the cultivation of this article, as they are before the
public by other and more able pens than mine. I
have spoken of cotton because it is the giant support of slavery, but I am quite in favour of ceasing to
use all slave-labour produce as soon as practicable.
Cuban sugar, so extensively used in England, is the

production of slave-labour, and not only does England support slavery by its use, but the slave-trade also. It is supposed that from 30,000 to 40,000 slaves are imported into Cuba annually who are engaged in the cultivation of sugar thus used. May God hasten the day when slavery shall be no more!

TESTIMONIALS.

Clayton Place, Kennington Road, London,
August 20, 1860.

My dear Sir,

I read and re-read your small work with deep attention and interest, and rejoice that in your forthcoming publication you are about to supply some authentic narratives of the perilous adventures and, in most instances, great sufferings of those who are courageous enough to leave the house of bondage for the home of freedom ; while I think your book will be a valuable addition to our Anti-Slavery literature, I am desirous that it should do more than merely furnish reading to the friends of the Slave. I earnestly wish it may excite such an active and liberal sympathy as may lead to the speedy contribution of the sum which is needed to enable you to accomplish the object of your mission, and then to return to that field of ministerial and benevolent labour which you have left behind you.

I can with confidence recommend you to the Abolitionists of Great Britain, having made myself acquainted with your credentials, knowing, also, that you are the authorized agent of the Free Mission Society, and that you possess the esteem and good opinion of those whom you represent in Canada. The work in which you are engaged is a most important one, both in connection with the welfare of those who are fortunate enough to escape from slavery into the British dominions, and the progressive improvement and elevation, morally and religiously, of the coloured community of Western Canada.

It is my sincere hope that through the publication of your "Underground Railroad," and your other efforts, your labours amongst us may be soon terminated by complete success, and that you may then, after a safe return to America, long live to succour the needy, instruct the ignorant, and advance the glorious cause of human emancipation.

Believe me, my dear Sir,

Very truly yours,

GEORGE THOMPSON.

Rev. W. Mitchell.

84, Newington Crescent, S.
19th August, 1860.

My dear Sir,

I have read with great interest the little book you have written, and are about to publish for the purpose of enlisting English sympathy on behalf of the Fugitive Slaves of America. The book contains the results of your own observations and experience, and is eminently calculated to accomplish the object you have in view. I hope, therefore, that your enterprise will receive the support of all our Anti-slavery friends, and of no small portion of the general public.

In conclusion, I must be allowed to pay my tribute to the earnestness and success of your labours in this country on behalf of your oppressed and suffering race.

Very truly yours,

F. W. CHESSON,
Hon. Sec. London Emancipation Committee.

Rev. W. Mitchell.

From WM. HOWARD DAY, Esq., M.A., of Chatham, Kent County,
Canada West.

4, America Square, Minories, London, E.C.,
August 20, 1860.

REV. WILLIAM M. MITCHELL.

Dear Brother,

I am happy to add a word to the numerous endorsements
already given you, as to the necessity of the work in which you
are engaged in Canada, and as to the earnestness which, from
personal knowledge, I can testify you exercise in that work.

More or less, since 1843, I have been in Canada among the
fugitive slaves, teaching and labouring otherwise for their
benefit. I have even travelled for three hundred miles on foot
from house to house, to visit these people in their homes. For
the last five years I have been a permanent resident among them,
and think, therefore, I know the people and their instructors.
And to you, who know me, I think I can say, without being
liable to the charge of attempting to flatter you, that among the
ministers in Canada, in direct contact with the coloured people, I
know of none who are preaching with more effect, and labouring
otherwise with more earnest desire to do good, than you.

Meeting you here, providentially, I have been pleased to
attend upon your meetings lately held, and in my humble way
otherwise to evince my earnest desire that you succeed in your
excellent object, viz.: to rear a chapel in the city of Toronto,
for the benefit of the coloured people, for the worship of the
Living God.

As a labourer in Canada, I may be permitted to say I do
earnestly hope that you may be soon enabled to return to your
interesting field of labour, laden with the practical sympathy of
this great country for the fugitive slave. The fewness of the
labourers renders this the more necessary, and your position in
the city of Toronto renders it more urgent still.

The book which you now bring forward as a means of enabling
you to accomplish your object, I have read and re-read with
great interest, not merely because it is full of thrilling facts, but

because I have been personally acquainted with some of the individuals named, and the facts detailed. I believe they are all what they pass for—facts. Perhaps it is easier for me to believe them so to be, because I have, as before stated, been conversant with those who have thus escaped by this "Underground Railroad." But a look into the prison-house of American bondage, and an acquaintance with its victims, will convince any that "Truth is stranger than fiction."

This work ought to be circulated, because it teaches the A B C of Anti-slavery, as well as its higher mathematics. There is need to again arouse the sentiment of this country as against chattelization, or human slavery; and as the pioneers are passing away—the men who achieved West India freedom—and as we become commercially more attached to the land of bondage, we need to indoctrinate anew the present generation. Thus commerce will not entirely stultify our national conscience; thus our supineness and indifference, induced mainly by the use of slave-labour cotton as opposed to cotton of free labour, will pass away, and the British heart again speak its true word against the enslavement of man.

This work by you, dear sir, is another evidence of what a man can accomplish who, like yourself, has had to acquire education, even in the face of almost insurmountable difficulties. The encouragement of this work will therefore be an encouragement to all such as are struggling against tremendous odds, and thereby a grand help to our grander cause.

In the best of bonds,

I remain,

Very truly for freedom,

WILLIAM HOWARD DAY.

It affords me much gratification to join with those esteemed friends who have already testified to Mr. Mitchell's claims being worthy of the sympathy and support of all Christian people. The cause in which he is engaged is a most important one—the service he is endeavouring to render to the fugitive slave population, one which has been long lost sight of ; and his credentials are such as must satisfy every one of his fitness for his work. I had the pleasure of hearing Mr. Mitchell address a large assembly the other evening, and can testify to his being a man of no ordinary ability.

ALEXANDER M. POLLOCK, A.M.,
Chaplain to his Excellency the Lord-Lieutenant.

Dublin, 9th April, 1859.

I can fully express my hope that the Christian friends in Dublin will cheerfully accord to Mr. Mitchell such proofs of their good-will as to enable him and his coloured brethren to hold on their way cheerfully in the good work of our common Lord.

W. URWICK, D.D.

Dublin, Ireland.

I have pleasure in adding my testimony to that of my highly-esteemed friend, Dr. Urwick; I have looked at Mr. Mitchell's credentials, which are many and strong; and having stopped myself some time at Toronto, I can well assert that the object he is endeavouring to carry out is one that deserves our Christian sympathy.

CHARLES M. FLEURY, D.D.,
Chaplain to his Excellency the Lord-Lieutenant.

Dublin, Ireland.

I have much pleasure in recommending Mr. Mitchell and his cause to the Christian public, as one deserving their sympathy.

The Hon. and Rev. BAPTIST W. NOEL.

London.

Mr. MITCHELL and his cause, with his much-esteemed and worthy companion, Rev. W. TROY, have been recommended to the sympathies of British Christians by the New Association for the Abolition of Slavery, Glasgow; and their reception by the Anti-slavery Societies in Ireland, Scotland, and England, for whom they have lectured, has been most satisfactory to them and the friends of humanity in this country.

Printed by Woodfall and Kinder, Angel Court, Skinner Street, London.

CPSIA information can be obtained
at www.ICGtesting.com
Printed in the USA
LVHW081633120619
621003LV00006B/109/P

9 780344 196959